Claus Oetke

Truth Paradoxes, Meaning, and Interpretation

Two Essays

Edited by

Wolfgang Künne and Ernst Steinkellner

ÖSTERREICHISCHE AKADEMIE DER WISSENSCHAFTEN
PHILOSOPHISCH-HISTORISCHE KLASSE
SITZUNGSBERICHTE, 921. BAND

Wolfgang Künne and Ernst Steinkellner (Eds.)

Claus Oetke
Truth Paradoxes, Meaning, and Interpretation

Two Essays

AUSTRIAN ACADEMY OF SCIENCES PRESS

This publication was subject to international and anonymous peer review. Peer review is an essential part of the Austrian Academy of Sciences Press evaluation process. Before any book can be accepted for publication, it is assessed by international specialists and ultimately must be approved by the Austrian Academy of Sciences Publication Committee.

The paper used in this publication is DIN EN ISO 9706 certified and meets the requirements for permanent archiving of written cultural property.

ISBN 978-3-7001-8880-3

Print: Prime Rate, Budapest
https://epub.oeaw.ac.at/8880-3
https://verlag.oeaw.ac.at
Made in Europe

Table of Contents

Editors' Notes

Claus Oetke (Jan. 3, 1947–Dec. 17, 2019) received his doctorate (1973) and postdoctoral qualification (1983) at the University of Hamburg, held a professorship at its *Institut für Kultur und Geschichte Indiens und Tibets* from 1983 to 1993, professorships on deputation in Kiel and Vienna, and a *Heisenberg Professur* of the *Deutsche Forschungsgemeinschaft* which led to visiting professorships at universities in the USA and Australia. From 1993 to 2014, he was head of the Section for Indology at the Department of Oriental Languages at Stockholm University. After his retirement he lived in Costa Rica.

One of his first publications was a book on philosophical issues of logic and linguistics, *Paraphrasenbeziehungen zwischen disjunktiven und konjunktiven Sätzen* (1981). He published numerous articles and monographs on Indian philosophies, mainly dialectics and logic, after his monumental *"Ich" und das Ich: Analytische Untersuchungen zur buddhistischen und brahmanischen Ātmankontroverse* (1998). In the Indian field, Nāgārjuna's Madhyamaka philosophy, the *trairūpya* logic, and Dharmakīrti's logic and theory of causality were his main interest.

The present volume contains two essays from Claus Oetke's literary estate, "Truth Paradoxes and Varieties of Meaning" and "Fact, Fake, and Fiction in Historical Interpretation", that he had planned to integrate into a book. Both essays are self-contained, but Oetke's Preface highlights their conceptual and argumentative connections.

The most elementary case of a truth paradox is generated if one assumes that somebody makes the statement 'What is asserted in this very utterance is not true'. By a reasoning that follows *prima facie* impeccable rules of derivation one arrives at the unacceptable conclusion that the sentence the speaker uttered expresses a truth if and only if it does not express a truth. Using the apparatus of classical logic (in the style of Gentzen's calculus of natural deduction) Oetke's first essay presents a variety of paradoxes that all deserve the title 'truth paradox' if one endorses his explanation of this title. In each case, he argues, the paradoxical conclusion can be avoided without putting blame on any principle of classical logic or on our pre-theoretical understanding of the predicate 'true'. What is really responsible for the conceptual embarrassment that arguments with paradoxical conclusions cause is rather a failure to take a certain kind of (truth-value bearing) content into consideration that can often be safely neglected. Oetke elaborates a distinction between (1^{a}) content as conventional lexico-grammatical meaning, "linguistic meaning" in his terminology, (1^{b}) content as something that is determined by lexico-grammatical meaning and certain elements of the context of an utterance, *and* (2) content as "holistic meaning". The need to distinguish between (1^{a}) and (1^{b}) is well known: utterances of indexical sentences like 'It's my 30th birthday today' made by different speakers or at different times can have different truth values (hence differ in content) in spite of having the same lexico-grammatical meaning. What is original with Oetke is the invocation of notion (2). The elucidation, and the application, of the concept of holistic meaning takes centre stage in the first essay in this book, for it is by bringing this kind of content into play that Oetke tries to (dis)solve all truth paradoxes.

This notion plays a key role not only in the contribution to the *philosophy of logic and of language* that the philosopher Oetke bequeathed to us in the form of the first essay, but also in his contribution to *hermeneutics* that the Indologist Oetke bequeathed to us in the form of the second essay.

An earlier version of this second essay under the title "The Fallacy of Historical Interpretation" was meant to continue a five-paper discussion on the *sadvitīyaprayoga* (the proof-formulation that entails a counterpart) which appeared between 2012 and 2016 in the *Journal of Indian Philosophy.* On April 20, 2016 Oetke informed E.S. in an e-mail that he wanted to submit the above paper for publication in the same journal. But the journal's editor added a note at the end of the last article in the series, "Final Notes on the *Sadvitīyaprayoga,*" in vol. 44 of 2016: "With the publication of this paper we hope to end this debate here. The Editor." In any case, on August 29, 2016, Oetke reported in a further e-mail to E.S. that he had tried to increase the interest of his paper not only by arguing with his opponent's last paper on the topic proper, but also by entering on more general questions of a theoretical and methodological nature. He also mentioned that he had not yet received either an answer or even an acknowledgement of receipt from the journal.

To all who knew Claus Oetke it can be no surprise that this silent indication of "enough is enough" stoked the fire of his brilliant mind. The second essay in this book is, therefore, a more expanded presentation of the thoughts he had offered in his contribution to the series on the *sadvitīyaprayoga*. Oetke is not only relentless in his critique of his opponent, but also critical of some of his own contributions to the series. Indeed, he goes far beyond them, discussing essential issues of methodology that are worth considering and deliberating for all who are concerned with documents of Indian or other philosophies, be it from a historical or philosophical point of interest.

We are deeply grateful to one of the anonymous evaluators for the Academy, who provided many helpful corrections, comments and suggestions for further improvement, and to Cynthia Peck-Kubaczek, who gave this book its final form.

Wolfgang Künne
em. Professor of Philosophy,
University of Hamburg

Ernst Steinkellner
em. Professor of Buddhist and
Tibetan Studies,
University of Vienna

Preface

This book combines two essays which, though differing in character and dealing with disparate issues, are united by a common topic and concern. While the second one focuses on matters of interpretation of a specific statement articulated in a certain philosophical tradition, the first one is dedicated to a purely theoretical problem. The central concern permeating both essays lies in propagating the relevance of acknowledging diverse types of meaning and, as corollary, distinct varieties of interpretation.

The connection between the topics of truth paradoxes and meaning consists in the fact that in the context of analysing truth paradoxes a schematic principle linking meaning to truth plays a pivotal role. It can be formulated as follows:

(T) [For any sentence s:] If s expresses that p then s thereby expresses a truth if and only if p.

(T) provides a link between meaning and truth on account of the fact that the question of what linguistic units express depends on their meaning(s). A significant subclass of sentences even permits to substitute 'expresses' by 'means' in (T). This principle obviously combines two subprinciples:

(T1) [For any sentence s:] If s expresses that p then s thereby expresses a truth *only if* p

(T2) [For any sentence s:] If s expresses that p then s thereby expresses a truth *if* p.[1]

---

[1] Or equivalently:

[For any sentence s:] If s expresses that p and s thereby expresses a truth then p.

[For any sentence s:] If (s expresses that p) and p, then s thereby expresses a truth.

The second subprinciple, (T2), plays a crucial role in all varieties of truth paradox considered in the first essay. If we deny its general validity we can maintain all logical rules that are employed in their derivation. It is possible to accommodate even (T2) to the intuition which presumably underlies its apparent plausibility if one replaces the relation the term 'express' signifies by a different but similar relation linking sentences to a type of content which does not coincide with the content they express in virtue of their linguistic meaning (or in virtue of their linguistic meaning together with certain features of the extra-linguistic context).

For some time now it has been customary to distinguish various semantic notions like reference ('*Bedeutung*') and sense ('*Sinn*') as conceived by Gottlob Frege and 'conventional significance' as conceived by Michael Dummett[2] which comes closest to the ordinary notion of (linguistic) meaning. According to the account of truth paradoxes that is proposed in the first essay, even in the realm of sentences without indexical elements (where Fregean sense and conventional significance coincide) an additional kind of content can be specified to which both (T1) and (T2) can be applied without leading to paradoxes and which seems to be a suitable candidate for the status of the bearer of absolute, not relativized, truth values. By this move the variety of semantic concepts is increased. Given that different semantic notions correlate with different types of interpretation, the variety of types of interpretation which are apt to attain relevance also increases. Now it may seem as if the need to appeal to the additional kind of content that licenses applications of both (T1) and (T2) remains restricted to quite 'exotic' cases where items expressing truth-value assessments refer to themselves or to other truth-value assessments. So, it comes as no surprise that historically oriented scholars (although some of them deal with rather exotic issues themselves) are sometimes inclined to infer from the outlandish nature of

---

2 Cf. M. Dummett, *The Interpretation of Frege's Philosophy*. (Harvard University Press) Cambridge/MA 1981, esp. 44, 77 and 99–104.

theoretically conceivable situations their irrelevance. But the appearance of a restriction to outlandish cases turns out to be deceptive if one takes a number of facts into account:

1) Although initially examples exhibiting obvious self-reference are most apt to strike the eye it turns out that similar phenomena can equally be detected among items which do not exhibit immediately noticeable self-reference. Accordingly, one should remain prepared for the possibility that deeper going investigations reveal that the area of relevant cases is far larger than initially supposed.

2) Ascriptions of truth or absence of truth obviously play a vital role in many contexts of life. Phenomena which are manifested by truth-value assessments in a particular domain may bring properties to light which pertain to all such assessments. Against this backdrop one cannot be offhand about the circumstance that particular specimens unveil differences capable of affecting the truth of truth-value assessments.

3) A dependence of the truth value of ascriptions of truth or absence of truth on semantic facts that are not linguistically expressed by them can be detected even in cases which do not belong to the specific group generating truth paradoxes. In the case of many ordinary truth assessments one can easily ascertain that the issue of whether linguistic items articulating them express a truth crucially relies on semantic properties belonging to different linguistic units, i.e. the question which truth value they have depends on the question of what other items mean or express.[3] The

[3] Essentially the same sort of dependence can be noticed in the realm of answers to questions, especially when made by saying 'Yes' or 'No'. It evidently depends on the content of a pertinent question whether or not answers given by using those words can be assessed as correct. Furthermore, under different circumstances the very same words can involve a difference of the kind of content that is asserted. Sometimes the content of those assertions can be also represented by expressions that result from transforming the questions into (complete) declarative sentences. (This latter

notion of a specific variety of content that can be regarded as a bearer of absolute truth without giving up either (T1) or (T2) takes account of this phenomenon.

4) The type of content for which principle (T) can be maintained as valid even with respect to items responsible for the origination of truth paradoxes exhibits the distinctive feature of potentially transcending both everything that is explicitly conveyed by words and the actual intentions of language users. Now the same characteristic is discernible even in connection with a category of truth-value appraisals which do not threaten to entail paradoxical conclusions. The very existence of this phenomenon, especially the fact that sometimes any attempt to ascertain the mental states of language users is entirely irrelevant, possesses significance for interpretation in general.

5) Even more important than all this is the fact that the enterprise of analysing problems posed by the occurrence of truth paradoxes gives rise to questions about meanings of a fundamentally different type — meanings that do not pertain to linguistic objects. Within the broad category of meanings ascribable to non-linguistic items a sub-category attains particular relevance here, namely meanings which are the topic of questions of the forms 'What does it mean for (an) X to be F?', 'What does (an) X's being F mean?', 'What does it mean that (an) X is F?' or more generally 'What does it mean that p?'. The plain observation that the placeholder 'X' can be replaced by terms denoting linguistic objects suffices for making obvious the potential relevance of those formulae even for linguistic matters. In addition to this, their prospective significance for the question of truth or untruth derives from the circumstance that the other placeholder, the letter 'F', can be substituted by 'true', 'express something which is true' or similar terms. As a matter of fact, questions of the type: 'What does it mean for s to be

form of answering questions whether things are thus and so is quite commonly employed in a number of languages and linguistic communities.)

true?' or, more explicitly 'What does it mean for s to express something which is true?', 'What does it mean that s says something true?', or 'What does it mean that s is used for saying something true?', where 's' is replaceable by a term referring to a linguistic object, play a pivotal role in the first essay in this book. Taking those questions into consideration assists in solving problems that arise from inconsistent truth-value ascriptions. Although the pertinent inconsistencies emerge only in very special cases, general significance can be ascribed to the fact that certain topics require or at least strongly suggest that one brings into play questions of meaning pertaining to linguistic items *and* issues of meaning pertaining to non-linguistic entities. Hence it is advisable to view the activity of interpretation as comprising, at least in principle, two different but closely linked types of investigation that focus on meanings of two different kinds. Settling questions concerning the meaning of linguistic objects and settling questions concerning the meaning of non-linguistic items both belong to the activity of interpretation — even if in particular contexts it can be legitimate to focus exclusively on one of these inquiries. The existence of different types of meaning and of different aspects of interpretation correlates with the fact that possible objects of *understanding* are not only linguistic units like sentences or texts, i.e. webs of sentences, but also non-linguistic entities, in particular objects expressible in language, such as theories, proofs, arguments etc. Carefully distinguishing the most fundamental varieties of meaning and interpretation enables us to recognize both the relevance and the limitations of philological enquiries which exclusively concern meaning of the first type. The tendency of some historically oriented scholars to ignore those varieties or to brush them aside as irrelevant made it mandatory to include some polemical passages in the second essay.

The topic which is elaborated in the first essay is touched upon for the sake of illustration in the second essay. Readers of the first essay are likely to raise the question whether, or in what respect, its main results might have a bearing on other less theoretical and less ‘exotic’ matters, in particular on historically orientated inquiries. The second essay answers this question affirmatively. In the first essay issues of meaning enter the limelight whereas the second essay deals primarily with interpretation. Because of the intimate connection between both kinds of issues we did not seek to avoid a certain overlap between both essays.

In the exploration of the varieties of truth paradox technical segments alternate with non-technical expositions. This phenomenon is due to the maxim that the treatment of this topic should be as non-technical as possible and as technical as necessary. As it is a major aim of the inquiry to precisely ascertain the principles and rules coming into play in the derivation of inconsistencies or other disconcerting outcomes, it was impossible to abstain from technical methods: they make involved presuppositions explicit to a maximal degree and thereby enable us to identify those factors which turn out to be most questionable. A short explanation of the employed derivation technique is presented in an appendix at the end of the first essay. Readers who are not (yet) acquainted with the employed techniques may find it helpful. The explanations of the pertinent rules of derivation should make it clear how well-entrenched the underlying intuitions are which would have to be disregarded if one were to dismiss any of these rules in order to preserve (T) in its original form, that is, in the form in which it does not take into account the need of invoking different types of content.

Part One

Truth Paradoxes and Varieties of Meaning

Abstract

The aim of this essay is to show 1) that there are various types of truth paradox exhibiting various kinds of *prima facie* unacceptable consequences derivable in a *prima facie* appropriate manner from *prima facie* indisputable assumptions, 2) that in all those cases the derivations rely on some shared principle(s) linking meaning to truth without which the seemingly indefensible results would not follow, 3) that considerations whose plausibility is not exclusively based on the fact that their acknowledgment would eliminate a basis for the derivation of paradoxical consequences support a dismissal, or rather a modification, of the crucial principle(s), 4) that, viewed in this light, truth paradoxes do not provide compelling reasons for rejecting established derivation rules of (classical) logic or for discarding common intuitions about truth and 5) that certain linguistic items can consistently be classified as untrue or even false which otherwise are apt to be regarded as falling into a truth-value gap.

It emerges as a result that, rather than putting into question ordinary intuitions about *truth*, truth paradoxes affect our conceptions about what linguistic items *mean*, what they express and what can be asserted by employing them and indirectly even concern the concept of translation. A major outcome of our investigation lies in the circumstance that it highlights the significance of raising questions about meaning which do not (directly) pertain to linguistic expressions. They are *not* represented by questions of the form 'What does E mean?', where 'E' is a placeholder for a term designating a (meaningful) linguistic item of any category and where 'mean' covers all varieties of meaning which linguistic expressions can exhibit. They are conveyed rather by questions of the forms 'What does being F mean?', 'What does it mean (for x) to be F?', or 'What does it mean that x is F?'

The present essay is not concerned with the issue whether particular *formal systems* permit one to derive as theorems statements engendering truth paradoxes or how the derivability of such theorems can be prevented.[4] It rather focuses on the question which consequences can or should be drawn from the fact that many *natural languages* permit the formulation of sentences which in virtue of their content are apt to generate truth paradoxes.

4 This question is dealt with in several publications on truth paradoxes: see, *inter alia*, Cook 2009:273ff.

I. Introductory Remarks

In the context of the present essay the term '*paradox*' is taken to apply *primarily* to *propositions* that exhibit the following characteristics: i) It appears *prima facie* impossible to consider them as true; ii) they result as consequences from *prima facie* undeniable assumptions by applying only principles of derivation whose validity seems indubitable. In a *secondary* sense the word is also used to characterize an *argument* the conclusion of which is a paradox in the primary sense or to a totality of assumptions and principles entailing a paradox in the primary sense or to an apparently impeccable derivation where the mere fact that the conclusion, although its truth is conceivable, should follow from the assumptions is utterly perplexing. The adjective 'paradoxical' can be applied not only to possible contents of linguistic items, in particular sentences, but also to the linguistic items themselves that represent the crucial consequences and principles of reasoning. In addition to this, the word can even be applied to the *fact* that *prima facie* unbelievable consequences can be deduced from apparently acceptable assumptions by apparently acceptable principles of reasoning.

The elucidation just given tallies with a quite common use of the expression 'paradox'. It is reflected, among others, in the explanation presented in Sainsbury 1988:1, according to which a paradox is 'an apparently unacceptable conclusion derived by apparently acceptable reasoning from apparently acceptable premises'. There are alternative proposals that differ from the one outlined above in various respects, e.g. by assigning the opposite priority ordering to the different employments of the term 'paradox'. But since these divergences are immaterial for the issues to be considered in this essay, we can confine ourselves to merely pointing out this fact without going into further details.[5]

One can make some general distinctions based on the character of the consequences which are classifiable as paradoxes. Thus we can classify a paradox (in the primary sense) as an 'antinomy' if and only if it consists in a proposition which is a formal contradiction (a sentence of the form 'p and not p').[6] We can use the expression 'logical paradox' with respect to situations where the truth of a derivable outcome can be regarded as impossible due to logical reasons even though it is not a formal contradiction, for example consequences of the form 'a is F if and only if a is not F'. Moreover (following Quine) a distinction can be drawn between 'veridical' paradoxes, cases in which the resulting consequence(s), notwithstanding (possible) appearance to the contrary, turn(s) out to be true as a result of deeper reflection, and 'non-veridical' or 'falsidical' paradoxes, where the consequence(s) cannot be established as true in the final analysis and might be even demonstrably false.[7] The subsequent investigations will suggest that the differences we just mentioned are by no means the only ones which are pertinent in this area.

Before presenting an explanation of the less comprehensive term '*truth paradox*' it is appropriate to introduce a notion which will be designated by the expression 'truth comment', or, for short, 'T-comment'. This expression will in the first place refer to any statement or vehicle of a statement which is or implies an ascription of truth or lack of truth to any item which could be regarded as a possible bearer of the property of being true. In an extended manner the term should encompass also cases where propositions are implied relating to possession or lack of truth as their component, for example statements to

[5] Künne 2013:40, footnote 66, points out that some authors consider as primary the usage which is treated here as extended or secondary. Regarding the possibility of a less restrictive employment of 'paradox', see M. Clark 2012:xi [2012:11] and 2012:159ff [2012:179ff]. — The numbers in squared brackets refer to the pages in the German edition.

[6] Cf. Künne 2013:40.

[7] Cf. Quine 1966:3ff.

the effect that something is true if and only if p, and similar ones. Whenever an apparently unacceptable or perplexing consequence can be derived in an apparently acceptable manner from a truth comment or a group of items to which a truth comment belongs such that the same consequence would no longer follow if among the assumptions at least one element which is a truth comment were dropped, we consider the consequence as a truth paradox, and in an extended sense we might call an entire argument exhibiting the corresponding quality — or even the fact that such an argument is possible — a 'truth paradox'. It is implicitly presupposed that the pertinent consequences in situations of truth paradox do not depend on any assumptions which are taken as untruths in the given context and that the premises constituting the basis of the derivation characterize situations whose possible existence can be plausibly assumed. In the present connection a most important fact is that the possibility for a proposition or an argument to qualify as a truth paradox does not require that the consequence relates in any manner to matters of truth, in particular that in a sentence expressing the consequence contains the expression 'true' or some synonymous term. Apart from the quality of appearing unacceptable with respect to the consequence it matters only that in the set of assumptions elements occur which exhibit the character of T-comments according to the preceding explanation of the term.

The concept of a truth paradox ought by itself not embody any prejudgment concerning the issue as to what are possible bearers of truth or which sorts of items are to be regarded as primary bearers of truth in the final analysis, and the preceding explanations should comply with this desideratum. At any rate, the elucidation presented above leaves room for many variations as far as the character of pertinent assumptions is concerned, in particular the character of premises which could be considered as T-comments. For example, assumptions of the form '(sentence) s is true', 's is untrue' as well as assumptions of the form 'NN said something true' or 'NN is right in asserting that p' etc. could (in principle) function as premises for the derivation of a truth paradox. The range of linguistic expressions which can be considered as T-comments is pretty diverse embracing, among others, expressions like a) 'yes', 'no', if the words are employed for claiming or disclaiming truth, b) expressions of the form 's expresses a truth', 'what s expresses is not true', where 's' relates to some linguistic item, c) 'A does not say anything which is true', 'what A said is true', where 'A' refers to a being capable of speaking a language. It deserves to be emphasized, on the other hand, that sentences or statements attributing the act of lying or the property of being a liar to an agent, or the property of being a lie to an utterance should not be regarded as members of the pertinent realm. The reason is that it is highly doubtful that lies have to be untruths.[8] Accordingly, we ought to reckon with the possibility that strictly speaking there are no liar paradoxes.

Although the area of truth comments and accordingly the potential realm of truth paradoxes is more encompassing, the subsequent exposition will draw the attention in the first place to situations where pertinent assumptions exhibit the forms of a) 'what s Φs is (not) true / is (not) a truth' and b) 's Φs something which is (not) true / is (not) a truth' or closely related ones, where 's' refers to a linguistic item, such as a sentence (token), and 'Φs' should be replaced by a verb signifying a relation between a linguistic unit and some (sort of) content associated with that unit, as for example 'expresses', 'conveys' etc. The reason lies in a supposition to the effect that the central results obtainable from considering these varieties of T-comment can be transferred to the whole realm.

Even under this provisional restriction a significant number of varieties have to be acknowledged due to the variation of the nature of the consequences qualified as truth paradoxes in what we have called the primary sense of this term. For this purpose, it is apposite to draw attention first to a pair of principles which appear at first glance pretty plausible. They have been recently presented in a version which relates to speakers of a language and read as follows:

8 See Künne 2013:24ff (chapter 1, §2) and Oetke 2013:11–12.

[P1] if (x says that p and x thereby says something which is true) then p.
[P2] if ((x says that p) and p) then x says something which is true.[9]

The intuition underlying these principles can be equally represented by two related principles which involve reference to linguistic items and might be formulated thus:

(TE1) [For any linguistic unit s:] if (s expresses that p and s thereby expresses a truth) then p.
(TE2) [For any linguistic unit s:] if (s expresses that p, and p) then s thereby expresses a truth.

These principles appear *prima facie* incontestable at least as far as sentences which are free from ambiguity are concerned.[10] If one acknowledges these prinicples it is most natural to accept two derivation rules as valid. The first rule licenses the deductive step from two assumptions to the effect that a linguistic unit expresses a truth and that it expresses that p (and nothing else) to the consequence that p. The second one legitimizes the step to the conclusion that some linguistic item expresses a truth from the assumptions that p and that the linguistic item in question expresses that p. In both cases the consequence would depend on no other assumptions than those on which the two assumptions depend (given that assumptions introduced

---

[9] Künne 2013:40. In the original German version they read:

[P1] wenn (x sagt, dass p, und x sagt damit etwas Wahres), dann p.

[P2] wenn (x sagt, dass p, und p), dann sagt x etwas Wahres.

The brackets in the English [P2] like the comma preceding '*und*' in the German original are to prevent the unintended reading 'x says that (p and p)'.

[10] The occurrence of 'thereby' is in fact dispensable with respect to items free of ambiguities. In Oetke 2012:253 the two principles had been obtained by the decomposition of a theorem which reads:

[For any linguistic unit s:] if s expresses that p, then s (thereby) expresses a truth if and only if p.

– The expression 'E*' occurring there (on p. 246 and later) has been replaced by 'E' in the present investigation and can be read as 'expresses something which is true'.

in a proof depend on themselves). Accordingly, one might specify the following rules of derivation which, even if they are not commonly mentioned as 'logical derivation rules', could perform analogous functions (the turnstile ⊢ can be read as 'therefore'):

(EE) s expresses a truth; s expresses that p ⊢ p
(EI) p; s expresses that p ⊢ s expresses a truth

The designations 'EE' ('*Expressing* Elimination') and 'EI' ('*Expressing* Introduction') are meant to reflect the circumstance that in the first case any reference to expressing a truth is 'eliminated' in the conclusion, whereas in the second case such reference is 'introduced'.[11]

[11] As one of the referees noted, these rules are valid if, and only if, substitution instances of 's' express exactly one proposition.

II. Types of Paradox

A) Simultaneous exhibition of or equivalence between truth and untruth

It seems feasible to deduce from premises which appear to represent possible facts a conclusion whose truth appears impossible to accept because it amounts to the supposition that one and the same (linguistic) item is both true and untrue, or that it both expresses a truth and fails to express a truth. In order to make as plain as possible the fact that the occurrence of this kind of situation is not affected by the question of whether one considers linguistic units as possible truth-value bearers or rather (non-linguistic) items which are in some manner related to linguistic units, we shall use the symbol 'E' in such a way that it may be interpreted either as 'is true' or as 'expresses a truth' (or in any sense which would be specified by replacing 'express' by any other term signifying a relation between linguistic entities and some sort of their content).

A rather straightforward — and familiar — way to derive an 'antinomy of truth' would be the following. Let 'Λ' designate the expression '¬ E Λ', where '¬' should be read as 'not' or 'it is not the case that' and where '¬ E Λ' means that the item designated by 'Λ' is not true or does not express a truth. This would seem to license the following steps of derivation[12]:

I)

1	(1)	E Λ	A(ssumption)
1	(2)	¬ E Λ	1 EE
1	(3)	E Λ & ¬ E Λ	1,2 &I
	(4)	¬ E Λ	1,3 RAA
	(5)	E Λ	4 EI

[12] For information about the style in which derivations are presented in this essay see the Appendix.

(6) $E \Lambda \& \neg E \Lambda$ 4,5 &I[13]

Alternatively, instead of (6) one could equally derive as a consequence:[14]

(6a) $E \Lambda$ if and only if $\neg E \Lambda$

Analogous consequences could be drawn without introducing stipulations concerning designations of linguistic units. A pertinent example, which reads

> 'Yields a falsehood when appended to its own quotation' yields a falsehood when appended to its own quotation.

is presented in Quine 1966:7.

This way of reasoning could be licensed by a maxim to the effect that from any (declarative) sentence an expression can be derived that results from replacing it by its own quotation or designation and attaching 'E' to it, and vice versa. Hence no (explicit) reference would be made to the idea of something which is expressed by linguistic items or which is related to them in some way as their content. On the other hand, if one directs one's attention to the question of the justification of that maxim, the idea of something which expressions possess as their content emerges in a most natural way, and (TE1) and (TE2) appear to provide the corresponding intuitive basis. This fact is vindicated by the following remarks occurring in Sainsbury 1988:119:

> Consider the sentence
> L_2. L_2 is not true.
>
> This is even more immediately paradoxical than L_1.[15] Suppose L_2 is true. Then it is as it says it is, viz., not true; so it is not true. However, suppose that it is not true. Well, *not true* is just what it says it is, and a sentence that tells it the way it is is true; so it is

13 'RAA' and '&I' refer to the rules of '*reductio ad absurdum*' and '&-introduction' respectively.

14 Cf. Bocheński/Menne 1973:93; Sainsbury 1988:114ff.

15 Sainsbury had introduced 'L1' on p. 114 as a designation of 'L1 is false'.

true. To sum up: If L_1 (*recte* L_2) is true, it is not true; if it is not true, it is true.

B) Conflicts with apparently incontrovertible assumptions concerning semantic content

Let us amplify the preceding sequence of derivational steps portrayed in I) by adding as an additional assumption a proposition to the effect that some sentence expresses with respect to itself that it is not true or that it fails to express anything which is true. This idea can be formulated as follows:

s expresses that not: E s

By permitting that the second occurrence of ‘s’ might be used referentially so that the particular way in which some sentence refers to itself is not essential one can consider this formulation as representing the ideas that some linguistic unit says or expresses about itself that it is not true or that it fails to express any truth — in accordance with the specific way one wants ‘E’ to be understood. There are various ways in which it could be achieved that a linguistic item attributes lack of truth or failure of expressing any truth to itself. It is not necessary to employ within a sentence any designation which one has arbitrarily assigned to that very sentence. One possibility lies in referring to linguistic tokens by using expressions of the form ‘the sentence which is uttered by NN at place P at time T (.....)’, such that the contextual features are specified to the extent that the individual token that is being produced is uniquely designated, and attaching to this singular term a predicate by which lack of truth or failure of expressing a truth is attributed. Another possibility is indicated by the Quinean strategy mentioned above. There is no need to explore various alternatives in more detail as long as it can be taken for granted that there is at least one way in which a linguistic item can self-ascribe lack of truth or failure of expressing a truth. The following derivation of a paradox requires merely this possibility.

II)

1	(1)	Σ expresses that ¬ E Σ	A
2	(2)	E Σ	A
1,2	(3)	¬ E Σ	1,2 EE
1,2	(4)	E Σ & ¬ E Σ	2,3 &I
1	(5)	¬ E Σ	2,4 RAA
1	(6)	E Σ	1,5 EI
1	(7)	E Σ & ¬ E Σ	5,6 &I
	(8)	Σ does not express that ¬ E Σ	1,7 RAA

Would it be justified to dismiss the relevance of this derivation because it is obtained from I) by merely adding an additional assumption and by incorporating the original steps of derivation in the new framework? To be sure, the additional assumption introduced in II) appears to make only explicit a possibility which is tacitly presupposed in I). But in contrast to I), the consequence that represents the paradox in II) is neither an antinomy nor some proposition one would be inclined to classify as a 'logical impossibility' in accordance with a natural understanding of that expression. It does not primarily pertain to the notion of truth, but to the issue of what linguistic units might be able to express, say or convey etc. The character of paradox results because the assumption of the first line seems to describe a possible situation and the derivation in its entirety seems to show that this possibility does not obtain. While the considerations in section A), specifically the reasoning displayed in I), are apt to arouse questions about our conception of truth, II) makes manifest that essentially the same argument could equally be understood as signalling a problem concerning meaning and in particular the relationship between meaning and truth.

Similar observations can be made against the background of items disclaiming truth with respect to themselves in 'indirect' ways, such as X's attributing truth to some unit Y which in its turn disclaims truth with respect to X.

II*)

Let us suppose:

Ψ: E Ω

Ω: $\neg$ E Ψ

Thus:

1	(1)	Ψ expresses that E Ω	A
2	(2)	Ω expresses that $\neg$ E Ψ	A
3	(3)	E Ψ	A
1,3	(4)	E Ω	1,3 EE
1,2,3	(5)	$\neg$ E Ψ	2,4 EE
1,2,3	(6)	E Ψ & $\neg$ E Ψ	3,5 &I
1,2	(7)	$\neg$ E Ψ	3,6 RAA
1,2	(8)	E Ω	2,7 EI
1,2	(9)	E Ψ	1,8 EI
1,2	(10)	E Ψ & $\neg$ E Ψ	7,9 &I
1	(11)	Not: Ω expresses that $\neg$ E Ψ	2,10 RAA
2	(12)	Not: Ψ expresses that E Ω	1,10 RAA

The upshot is that either the assumption of line 1 or the assumption of line 2 cannot represent a truth, leaving open the possibility that both are untrue. This appears disconcerting because one should suppose that, in view of what has been stipulated at the beginning, it is both the case that Ψ expresses that Ω expresses something true, represented by 'E Ω', and that Ω expresses that Ψ fails to express a truth, represented by '$\neg$ E Ψ'. To be sure, the supposition that some (linguistic) item should ascribe to itself lack of truth or failure of expressing a truth appears unfamiliar. But one can hardly detect any plausible basis for the view that such self-ascriptions are impossible in principle. Be this as it may, the situation envisaged in II*) shows that the existence of apparently disconcerting consequences pertaining to matters of semantics does not essentially depend on the question of the possibility of direct self-reference and self-ascription. Furthermore, it should be noted that the exact import of the word 'express' or of any other term used to designate the pertinent relation does not matter for this argument. One might replace the word 'express' by some variable term, say 'ϕs', and write 'Ψ ϕs that E Ω' (instead of 'Ψ expresses that E Ω') and 'Ω ϕs that ¬E Ψ' (instead of 'Ω expresses that ¬E Ψ'), under the supposition that 'x ϕs y' designates any appropriate relation holding between (linguistic) units and contents representing truth ascriptions or truth denials: The derivability of a formal contradiction vindicates the impossibility of two items, such that one represents a truth ascription to some (different) item which in its turn represents a truth denial with respect to the former. Here the question whether the word 'express' is an appropriate term for signalling the pertinent relation between expressions and contents is not decisive.

C) Inconsistencies implied by apparently consistent suppositions regarding possible arrangements of T-comments

Let us suppose that there is some (actually) infinite series of T-comments, such that each member of the series denies truth with respect to all members subsequent to it. A series of this sort can be represented by various formulations, e.g. by

(a) A1: All subsequent items express an untruth, A2: All subsequent items express an untruth, A3: All subsequent items express an untruth, … …

(a*) A1: All subsequent items fail to express something true, A2: All subsequent items fail to express something true, A3: All subsequent items fail to express something true, … …

(b) B1: No subsequent item is true/expresses a truth, B2: No subsequent item is true/expresses a truth, B3: No subsequent item is true/expresses a truth, … …

(b*) B1: There is no subsequent item which expresses a truth, B2: There is no subsequent item which expresses a truth, B3: There is no subsequent item which expresses a truth, … …

Against this background one can reason as follows:

III)

(1) Let us assume that any member M of the series, which could be the very first or any subsequent item, expresses a truth.

(2) Then it must be true that every member subsequent to M is untrue/fails to express a truth.

(3) Therefore the immediately succeeding member M+1, as well as all items following it, are untrue/fail to express a truth.

(4) Since M+1, as well as all following items, express that all following items are untrue/fail to express a truth, it must be untrue that all members subsequent to M+1 are untrue.[16]

(5) Consequently there must be some member subsequent to M+1 that expresses a truth.

(6) This result militates against the consequence, formulated in (2), implied by the pertinent assumption, formulated in (1).

(7) Hence M must be untrue/fail to express a truth.

(8) Since M expresses that all subsequent members are untrue/fail to express a truth, it must be untrue that all members subsequent to M are untrue/fail to express a truth.[17]

(9) There must be some member M+N following M which expresses a truth.

(10) The reasoning demonstrating the impossibility of M's truth can be applied to M+N establishing that both the assumption of M's truth and M's absence of truth entail contradictions.

---

16 Or alternatively: Since M+1, as well as all following items, express that no following item is true/expresses a truth, it must be untrue that no member subsequent to M+1 is true/expresses a truth.

17 Or alternatively: Since M expresses that no subsequent member is true/expresses a truth, it must be untrue that no member subsequent to M is true/expresses a truth.

The case under consideration and the above presented piece of reasoning are based on the so-called 'Yablo-Paradox' about which it has been claimed (by its inventor) that it does not involve any self-reference.[18] At this point it is not needed to go into the details of the discussions about that claim. It should suffice to remark that some sort of self-reference is in fact involved inasmuch as the term 'subsequent' in (a)–(b*) represents a relational notion equivalent to 'subsequent to this', where 'this' refers to the item within which it occurs. However, there is no intuitive basis for claiming that III) involves a self-reference of the kind that can be discerned in II) or II*), where a T-comment appears to involve a direct or indirect comment on itself. But one could dispute the relevance of the considered example by maintaining that it militates against the previous requirement that truth paradoxes ought to exhibit the characteristic that apparently unacceptable consequences arise out of possible situations, for it is doubtful that the existence of an (actually) infinite series of linguistic items is possible. It has to be admitted, of course, that the supposition of the occurrence of an infinite sequence of linguistic items does not represent a realistic possibility, according to an intuitive understanding of the expression 'realistic possibility'. But one should not go so far as to deny that the envisaged possibility can 'in principle' be realized, for the pertinent assumption does not seem to involve an inconsistency. Nevertheless, this defence will not meet with universal assent, for it can be maintained that the concept of an 'actual infinity' is flawed in some other way than by being inconsistent.

One must indeed admit that the same paradoxical consequences would not arise if the situation of a *finite* series of subsequent truth denials (of any length) were considered — so that one might distinguish between 'infinite Yablo sequences' and 'finite Yablo sequences'. If one orientates oneself by the formulations employed in (b) and (b*) this is obvious: The very last member of any finite Yablo sequence should express a truth so that any previous member can be relegated to the realm of untruths. As far as (a) and (a*) are concerned,

[18] Cf. Yablo 1993:251–252 as well as Clark 2012:267ff [2012:292ff].

ordinary intuitions might waver with respect to the question whether one ought to classify a statement referring to all subsequent members as true or not, if no such members exist. Anyhow, if truth were denied one might consistently attribute truth to the penultimate member and failure of expressing a truth to the preceding members.[19] Against this background it is important to note that similar predicaments as in cases of infinite Yablo sequences can be discerned by considering slight modifications of finite Yablo sequences, such as:

> C1: All subsequent items fail to express a truth, C2: All subsequent items fail to express a truth, C3: All subsequent items fail to express a truth, C4: The immediately preceding item expresses a truth.

A pertinent piece of reasoning might proceed as follows:

IV)

(1) Let us suppose that C1 expresses a truth.

(2) Then C2, C3 and C4 fail to express a truth.

(3) Then C3 must express a truth because it would express a truth about C4. Thus a contradiction results.

(4) Let us instead assume that C1 fails to express a truth. Then C2, C3 or C4 must express a truth.

(5) If C2 expresses a truth then both C3 and C4 must fail to express a truth. But then C4 must express a truth so that an inconsistency results.

(6) If C3 expresses a truth then C4 must fail to express a truth, so that C3 fails to express a truth and an inconsistency results.

(7) If C4 expresses a truth then C3 expresses a truth so that C4 must fail to express a truth and an inconsistency arises again.

(8) Accordingly, C1 cannot fail to express a truth either.

---

19 The circumstance that, by hypothesis, all members exhibit the same formulation does not refute this possibility because the identity of linguistic content does not necessitate the identity of the type of content which is relevant for truth evaluation. (More about this will be said later.)

Obviously the state of affairs would not be substantially altered if additional items exhibiting the same formulation as C3 were inserted immediately before the ultimate member of the series. The crucial factor is that the relationship between C3 and C4 is exactly like that between Ω and Ψ in II*). Thus self-reference plays an important role in the considered modification of finite Yablo sequences. But the predicament that both assumptions of truth and of absence of truth lead to inconsistencies here affects even elements which do not occur as (direct or indirect) objects of T-comments, such as C1.

These observations cannot refute the thesis that all invocations of an infinity of related T-comments entail special problems. For the time being, this issue need not be pursued and can be taken up later. What matters here and now is that in the preceding expositions of pieces of reasoning both the principle represented by '[P1]', '(TE1)' or 'EE', and the principle represented by '[P2]', '(TE2)' and 'EI' come into play. The first one supports, for example, the steps from (1) to (2) in III) and in IV). And the reasoning in (4) and (8) within III) as well as that in (3) and (4) within IV) appeals to the second principle. For the theorem:

If s expresses that p then (if p then E s)

is equivalent to:

If s expresses that p then (if ¬ E s then ¬ p).

D) Derivability of contingent (historical) propositions from assumptions solely relating to non-contingent matters

Let us suppose that 'Γ' and 'Δ' designate respectively the expressions:

'E Δ'

and (with 'p →q' for 'if p then q')

'E Γ → Napoleon Bonaparte was an orthodox Hindu'

This amounts to a conditional attribution of truth on the part of one of the expressions, viz. 'Δ', to another expression, viz. 'Γ', saying that if it, viz. 'Γ', expresses a truth, then Napoleon Bonaparte was an orthodox Hindu. The same effect could be achieved by a sequence of two sentences, such that the first reads:

> The (immediately) subsequent sentence expresses a truth.

and the second:

> If the (immediately) preceding sentence expresses a truth, then Napoleon Bonaparte was an orthodox Hindu.

Let us use 'N' as an abbreviation for 'Napoleon Bonaparte was an orthodox Hindu'. Applied to the pertinent example the principles (TE1) and (TE2) run as follows.

With respect to Γ:

> If Γ expresses that E Δ & E Γ, then E Δ
> If Γ expresses that E Δ & E Δ, then E Γ

and with respect to Δ:

> If Δ expresses that [E Γ → N] & E Δ, then E Γ → N
> If Δ expresses that [E Γ → N] & E Γ → N, then E Δ

In the following arrangement of derivational steps those states-of-affairs will be introduced as assumptions and the sequence can be presented as follows:

V)

1	(1)	(Γ expresses that E Δ & E Γ) → E Δ	A
2	(2)	(Γ expresses that E Δ & E Δ) → E Γ	A
3	(3)	(Δ expresses that [E Γ → N] & E Δ) → (E Γ → N)	A
4	(4)	(Δ expresses that [E Γ → N] & (E Γ → N)) → E Δ	A
5	(5)	Γ expresses that E Δ	A
6	(6)	Δ expresses that [E Γ → N]	A
7	(7)	E Γ	A
5,7	(8)	Γ expresses that E Δ & E Γ	5,7 &I
1,5,7	(9)	E Δ	1,8 MPP
1,5,6,7	(10)	Δ expresses that [E Γ → N] & E Δ	6,9 &I
1,3,5,6,7	(11)	E Γ → N	3,10 MPP

1,3,5,6,7	(12) N	7,11 MPP
1,3,5,6	(13) $E\,\Gamma \rightarrow N$	7,12 CP
1,3,5,6	(14) Δ expresses that $[E\,\Gamma \rightarrow N]$ & $(E\,\Gamma \rightarrow N)$	6,13 &I
1,3,4,5,6	(15) $E\,\Delta$	4,14 MPP
1,3,4,5,6	(16) Γ expresses that $E\,\Delta$ & $E\,\Delta$	5,15 &I
1,2,3,4,5,6	(17) $E\,\Gamma$	2,16 MPP
1,2,3,4,5,6	(18) N	13,17 MPP

One could, but need not, continue as follows:

1,2,3,4,5,6	(19) $E\,\Delta \rightarrow N$	15,18 CP
1,3,5,6,7	(20) $\neg$ N	A
1,3,5,6	(21) $\neg\, E\,\Gamma$	13,20 MTT
1,3,5,6	(22) $\neg\, E\,\Delta$	19,20 MTT
1,3,4,5,6	(23) $E\,\Gamma$ & $\neg\, E\,\Gamma$	17,21 &I
1,3,4,5,6	(24) $E\,\Delta$ & $\neg\, E\,\Delta$	15,22 &I
1,2,3,4,5,6	(25) Not: Δ expresses that $[E\,\Gamma \rightarrow N]$	6,23/24 RAA
1,2,3,4,5,6	(26) Not: Γ expresses that $E\,\Delta$	5,23/24 RAA[20]

The final outcome of the extended version of V) closely resembles that of II), and in particular II*): It is impossible to satisfy all stipulations concerning the contents expressed by Γ and Δ. The result depends, however, on the contingent circumstance, that the state of affairs described by 'N', viz. that Napoleon Bonaparte was an orthodox Hindu, does not obtain. In contrast, the final conclusion of the non-extended version, formulated in line (18), solely depends on the original assumptions in lines (1)–(6). The thought that a historically untrue proposition should be derivable from those assumptions is perplexing. For the first line stipulates that if the item designated by 'Γ' expresses (or means) that the item designated by 'Δ' expresses a truth, then it holds true that if the item designated by 'Γ' in fact expresses a truth, then the term designated by 'Δ' also expresses a truth.[21] Similarly the

[20] 'MPP', 'CP' and 'MTT' designate the rules of '*modus ponendo ponens*', 'conditional proof' and '*modus tollendo tollens*' respectively.

[21] This paraphrase is legitimate because '$(p \,\&\, q) \rightarrow r$' is equivalent to '$p \rightarrow (q \rightarrow r)$'.

third line stipulates that if the item designated by 'Δ' expresses that if the item designated by 'Γ' expresses a truth then Napoleon Bonaparte was an orthodox Hindu, then it must hold true that if the item designated by 'Δ' expresses a truth then it must be the case that if the item designated by 'Γ' expresses a truth then Napoleon Bonaparte was an orthodox Hindu. This amounts to an application of the idea that if some (linguistic) item L expresses that p, then it holds good that if L (thereby) expresses a truth, then it is the case that p. On the other hand, the lines 2 and 4 represent applications of the idea that if something expresses something or other, then it holds good that if what is thereby expressed is a truth then the item expressing it expresses a truth. Since those two ideas appear like truisms, at least as long as items that are free of ambiguities are concerned, it is hard to believe that they should constitute a basis for deriving false contingent propositions. As the subsequent lines (5) and (6) merely represent the pertinent stipulations concerning the expressed content (or the meaning) of the items designated by 'Γ' and 'Δ', it appears perplexing that they in combination with the remaining assumption of (1)–(4) enable the derivation of an untrue proposition concerning contingent historical matters. But that is not all: One can easily see that by the method of V)(1)–(18) it would be possible to derive *any* arbitrary (true or untrue) proposition. One would only have to replace 'N' by some other item — or bestow on the letter 'N' a different interpretation than before. Instead of employing 'EE' and 'EI' as derivation rules, the applications of the underlying principles have been introduced as assumptions in lines (1)-(4), for in this manner it becomes particularly conspicuous that the possible derivation of arbitrary propositions needs to rely only on most elementary derivation rules, specifically '&I' and 'MPP'.

A derivation possessing a similar effect has been presented in Künne 2013:55–57 against the background of the assumption that some Cretan says or asserts that all Cretans assert nothing but untruths. The sequence of derivational steps is as follows[22]:

VI)

1	(1)	$K[\forall x\,(Kx \rightarrow Fx)]$	A
2	(2)	$W[\forall x\,(Kx \rightarrow Fx)]$	A
2	(3)	$\forall x\,(Kx \rightarrow Fx)$	2; W-elimination
2	(4)	$K[\forall x(Kx \rightarrow Fx)] \rightarrow F[\forall x(Kx \rightarrow Fx)]$	3; $\forall$-elimination
1,2	(5)	$F[\forall x(Kx \rightarrow Fx)]$	1,4; MPP
1	(6)	$W[\forall x\,(Kx \rightarrow Fx)] \rightarrow F[\forall x(Kx \rightarrow Fx)]$	2,5; CP[23]
1	(7)	$W[\forall x(Kx \rightarrow Fx)] \rightarrow \neg W[\forall x(Kx \rightarrow Fx)]$	6; substitution $\neg$W/F
1	(8)	$\neg W[\forall x\,(Kx \rightarrow Fx)]$	7; Consequentia Mirabilis
9	(9)	$W[\forall x\,(Kx \rightarrow Fx)] \vee F[\forall x\,(Kx \rightarrow Fx)]$	A
1,9	(10)	$F[\forall x\,(Kx \rightarrow Fx)]$	8,9; Disjunctive Syllogism
9	(11)	$K[\forall x\,(Kx \rightarrow Fx)] \rightarrow F[\forall x\,(Kx \rightarrow Fx)]$	1,10; CP

The intended interpretation of the symbol ‘K’ is ‘is asserted by a Cretan’, ‘W’ and ‘F’ abbreviate the German counterparts of ‘is true’ and ‘is false’ (or ‘is not true’) respectively, and square brackets surrounding a sentence are used to form a singular term designating what is said by that sentence. Now according to (10), the assertion of a Cretan to the effect that Cretans assert only untruths cannot be true, given (1) that such an assertion was actually made and (9) that what was asserted is either true or false (not true). So, it has to be granted that, if the event of a Cretan’s attributing untruth to all assertions made by Cretans actually occurred, there must be some *different* assertion made by a Cretan which is not false (untrue). Although it is highly probable that on a different occasion some Cretan has indeed asserted something else that was true, the idea that this contingent

---

22 Künne’s entries on the right-hand side of lines (8) and (10) invoke theorems of the propositional calculus in order to abbreviate the derivation. The theorem appealed to in (8) is ‘$(p \rightarrow \neg p) \rightarrow \neg p$’, the theorem appealed to in (9) is ‘$((p \vee q) \,\&\, \neg p)) \rightarrow q$’.

23 Since it is line (2) that contains the discharged assumption, I took the liberty of replacing Künne’s entry ‘1,5; $\leftrightarrow$ Einführung (= CP)’ by ‘2,5; CP’.

fact should be guaranteed just by the circumstance that an (untrue) assertion of the described kind has been made, appears very astonishing.

In some respect the paradox generated by VI) is weaker than the puzzles which can be distilled from V), for they demonstrate that any arbitrary true or untrue proposition can be derived relying only on basic rules of derivation.

E) Imposed partiality of truth-value assignments

Let us consider the following argument:

VII)

1	(1)	H expresses that $\neg E \Theta$	A
2	(2)	Θ expresses that $\neg E H$	A
3	(3)	$E H$	A
1,3	(4)	$\neg E \Theta$	1,3 EE
5	(5)	$\neg E \Theta$	A
1,5	(6)	$E H$	1,5 EI
7	(7)	$E \Theta$	A
2,7	(8)	$\neg E H$	2,7 EE
9	(9)	$\neg E H$	A
1,9	(10)	$E \Theta$	2,9 EI
1	(11)	$E H \rightarrow \neg E \Theta$	3,4 CP
1	(12)	$\neg E \Theta \rightarrow E H$	5,6 CP
2	(13)	$E \Theta \rightarrow \neg E H$	7,8 CP
2	(14)	$\neg E H \rightarrow E \Theta$	9,10 CP
1	(15)	$(E H \rightarrow \neg E \Theta) \,\&\, (\neg E \Theta \rightarrow E H)$	11,12 &I
2	(16)	$(E \Theta \rightarrow \neg E H) \,\&\, (\neg E H \rightarrow E \Theta)$	13,14 &I
1,2	(17)	$(E H \leftrightarrow \neg E \Theta) \,\&\, (E \Theta \leftrightarrow \neg E H)$	15,16 &I[24]

The point can be illustrated by the following example.

---

24 ‘ ’ for ‘if and only if’. We have abstained from presenting a slightly shorter argument that applies the rule of ‘*modus tollendo tollens*’.

Let us imagine a situation where two persons A and B are colleagues who participate in some conference. Let us further suppose that the sentences

(U1) Not a single truth is said by my colleague B during this conference.

(U2) Not a single truth is said by my colleague A during this conference.

are assertively uttered by A and by B respectively and that those utterances constitute the only contributions of A and B to the pertinent conference.[25] Surely, these assumptions depict a possible situation. It is easy to verify that, at least according to ordinary intuitions concerning truth and saying something true, it is both impossible that both utterances express a truth and that both utterances express an untruth.[26] In accordance with (TE1) truth of (U1) implies untruth of (U2) and vice versa. An assumption of untruth with respect to one of them would imply the truth of the other one according to (TE2). The only consistent ways of attributing truth appear either an assignment of truth to (U1) and of lack of truth to (U2) or, the other way around, an attribution of truth to (U2) and of untruth to (U1). That in itself is not inconsistent. Consistency could be maintained even with respect to two utterances of a sentence obtained from (U1) and (U2) by deleting the names 'B' and 'A' respectively, since the occurrence of the indexical element ('my') allows for differences of (propositional) content. The crux lies rather in the fact that opting for one of the two opposing truth-assignments would be utterly arbitrary. It would be of no value to appeal to possible differences of reputation concerning the speakers of (U1) and (U2), for attributions of truth or

[25] Although the assumption that (during the conference) neither A nor B says anything else *which is true* would suffice for the subsequent exposition, the suggestion that (U1) and (U2) are the only contributions made by the two colleagues is proposed in order to underscore the similarity between the members of the pair.

[26] Here 'express a truth (an untruth)' stands for the more cumbersome formulation 'are used to say something that is true (not true)'.

untruth to individual statements should in the final analysis depend on what is said and not on the question who said it.[27] Is there a way of avoiding unfounded partiality and of substantiating the judgement that (U1) and (U2) deserve exactly the same verdict?

Quite similar observations can be made if one considers an infinite series of truth denials, where each member disputes truth with respect to its immediately subsequent member. If the initial member expressed a truth the immediately following member must fail to express a truth. But then — if one accepts (TE2) — the third member would express a truth, and so on. Apparently, however, no basis exists for preferring this way of assigning truth values against the alternative, where lack of truth is assigned to the initial member, possession of truth to the second, absence of truth to the third, and so on. If the series were finite the situation would be different: In accordance with the evaluation of the final member truth-assignments of the preceding items could be determined. To be sure, the situation would change again if the last member expressed a negative comment on a preceding element of the series.

It might appear tempting to solve the dilemma by maintaining that truth of a T-comment requires the existence of some item which is not a T-comment and which constitutes either a direct or at least an indirect object of the pertinent T-comment, as illustrated by:

(T)

T0: T1 does not express a truth.
T1: Napoleon Bonaparte made war on Prussia.

(T*)

T0: T1 does not express a truth.
T1: T2 expresses a truth.
T2: T3 expresses a truth.
T3: Napoleon Bonaparte made war on Prussia.

---

[27] Even those who think otherwise would be led into an impasse by the (not unrealistic) assumption that the speakers of (U1) and (U2) deserve the same degree of respect or disrespect.

But for various reasons one should be reluctant to adopt this 'solution':

1. One would have to assume that in a finite sequence like

(T)**

T0: The following remark is true.
T1: No subsequent item expressing a truth occurs.[28]

T0 could not be assessed as true, although intuitions support the view that here both T0 and T1 express something that is true.

2. In a sequence such as

(T*)**

T0: The subsequent remark is true.
T1: The preceding sentence either expresses a truth or fails to do so.

it would be more in accordance with ordinary intuitions to attribute truth to T0 than to consider it as untrue — or as neither true nor false.

3. With respect to a sequence like

(T**)**

T0: The subsequent remark expresses a truth.
T1: If the preceding sentence expresses a truth then Napoleon Bonaparte made war on Prussia.

— which is reminiscent of the situation envisaged in V) — intuitions do not license a sweeping rejection of the supposition that T0 expresses something true. It appears even more counterintuitive to deny T0 any assertible content. It seems, after all, that T0 can serve as a basis for derivations.

4. Let us grant for the sake of argument that both (U1) and (U2) above lack truth or even fail to assert anything. But aren't we impelled to admit that precisely under such circumstances both (U1) and (U2) tells it the way it really is?

These considerations should yield a sufficient motivation for seeking after alternative solutions.

---

28 Or alternatively: 'If there is any subsequent item, then it does not express a truth'.

III. Truth of T-comments

It is not difficult to ascertain that a great number of different arguments and considerations engendering paradoxes rely on exploitations of the principles (TE1) and (TE2) — or of variants that essentially come to the same thing as these principles. (TE1), viz.

> [For any linguistic unit s:] If s expresses that p and s thereby expresses a truth then p

appears incontrovertible, and the same holds for every suitable substitution instance of the schema

> If s ϕs that p and s thereby ϕs a truth, then p.

Since something can be related in the same way to different items, it may be apposite to distinguish a weaker and a stronger reading of the conjunct 's expresses a truth' in the antecedent of (TE1). According to the weaker reading it amounts to the same as

> s expresses something which is a truth.

According to the stronger reading the phrase is equivalent to

> s expresses nothing but a truth

or more explicitly

> s expresses something which is a truth and there is nothing expressed by s which is not a truth.

In the formulation of (TE1) that was initially presented the expression 'thereby' was inserted under the supposition that the weaker reading might be attributed to 's expresses a truth'. If, however, the stronger reading is assumed the addition is dispensable. As mentioned earlier, the difference between the alternative readings becomes immaterial whenever it can be supposed that an item is not simultaneously related to different contents in the way signalled by the term 'expresses' (or similar ones). Hence, if duly explicated, (TE1), at least as long as the linguistic unit s does not contain indexical elements, appears incontrovertible.

As far as (TE2), viz.

> [For any linguistic unit s:] If ((s expresses that p) and p), then s thereby expresses a truth.

is concerned, the constituent 'thereby' in the consequent clause is required only if, with respect to this clause, the stronger reading is envisaged and could be omitted otherwise. Even here the difference can be neglected if one does not have to account for the possibility that a pertinent item expresses different propositions. Thus the phenomenon of ambiguity does not suffice to discredit the validity of (TE1) and (TE2) but calls at most for suitable explications. Even if one would speak in a less explicit manner of truth and lack of truth with respect to *sentences* — instead of truth or lack of truth of something expressed or conveyed etc. by linguistic items — the difference can be accounted for by expressions like 'is true under some reading', 'is true under all (admissible) readings', 'is untrue/fails to be true under some reading', 'is untrue/fails to be true in under all (admissible) readings' or — to account for the possibility that some item is devoid of sense and admissible readings — 'does not possess any reading under which it is true'.

Given that (TE1) and (TE2) come into play in a great variety of considerations and derivations leading to or involving paradoxes and that (TE1) appears most incontrovertible, the conjecture suggests itself that in the final analysis (TE2) — as well as [P2] and the derivation rule 'EI' — have to be abandoned. From a merely formal viewpoint a derivation of the untruth of specific instances of (TE2) and the non-validity of (TE2) as a general principle could be easily accomplished. For example, instead of adding in argument V) after line (23) and (24) the final lines (25) and (26), conveying that at least one of the pertinent expressions cannot express that which they were supposed to express, one could add:

1,3,4,5,6,20	(25*)	Not: ((Γ expresses that E Δ) & E Δ) $\rightarrow$ E Γ	2,23/24 RAA
1,2,3,5,6,20	(26*)	Not: ((Δ expresses that [E $\Gamma \rightarrow$ N]) & [E $\Gamma \rightarrow$ N]) $\rightarrow$ E Δ	4,23/24 RAA

This amounts to claiming that if one a) maintains that the concerned items in fact express that which they were supposed to express, b) accepts the validity of (TE1) with respect to the pertinent case and c) takes it that Napoleon Bonaparte was in fact not an orthodox Hindu, then at least one of the instantiations of (TE2) must fail to be true. Similarly, by a minor transformation of I), which reads:

I')

1	(1)	E Λ	A
2	(2)	$\neg$ E $\Lambda \rightarrow$ E Λ	A
1	(3)	$\neg$ E Λ	1 EE
1	(4)	E Λ & $\neg$ E Λ	1,3 &I
	(5)	$\neg$ E Λ	1,3 RAA
2	(6)	E Λ	2,5 MPP
2	(7)	E Λ & $\neg$ E Λ	5,6 &I
	(8)	Not: $\neg$ E $\Lambda \rightarrow$ E Λ	2,7 RAA

it would convey that the instance of (TE2) that is represented in line (2) must be unconditionally rejected. Analogous arrangements could be made in II), II*) and in other cases.

At this point one faces an objection based on familiar considerations. It runs as follows:

> It is absolutely illegitimate to contest (TE2). For compliance with the antecedent clause in (TE2) means that things really are as we, by using the pertinent (linguistic) item, say they are, or that things are as the item in question says they are. But this can only mean that the concerned linguistic entity expresses a truth.[29]

Although the considered suspension of (TE2) need not entail a global rejection of its validity but merely an abrogation in special cases, it is

[29] Cf. also Künne 2003:334.

apposite to raise the general question of what it may mean that things really are as some linguistic unit, in particular a declarative sentence, says they are and that it accordingly expresses a truth. Let us first examine the issue by considering a sentence which is not a T-comment. Suppose that 'Π' designates the English sentence:

'Napoleon Bonaparte made war on Prussia'

The question as to what it means, in the envisaged sense of the word, that things are as Π says they are and that accordingly Π expresses a truth, suggests the following answer. It means at least two things, namely:

(a) that the English sentence 'Napoleon Bonaparte made war on Prussia' (in fact) expresses a truth

and

(b) that it is a truth that Napoleon Bonaparte made war on Prussia.

In this context 'that p means that q' amounts to the same as 'it cannot be the case that p unless it is the case that q'. The component (a) arises as a most immediate consequence because, trivially, something can only be the case if it is the case. (b) on the other hand must also be regarded as an indispensable requirement for the truth of Π: If it should be the case that (a) is satisfied it must equally hold good that something exists that is expressed by Π and which is a truth or which is true; given however, that the proposition that Napoleon Bonaparte made war on Prussia is the only conceivable content which can be rated as something that is linguistically expressed by Π, the truth of this content needs to constitute an indispensable condition for expressing a truth on the part of Π. The conjunction of (a) and (b) represents a necessary, and presumably sufficient, condition for Π's expressing a truth.

An application of the same principle to Λ in I) yields the following result:

Λ's expressing a truth means, that is, requires

(a) that Λ in fact expresses a truth

and

(b) that (it is a truth that) Λ fails to express a truth,

hence it requires the satisfaction of a contradiction, provided that Λ expresses precisely a denial of the proposition specified in (a). Since Λ does involve such a denial it can be deduced that the content specified in (b) should not establish Λ's truth; as it is the content which Λ expresses, Λ implies even a denial of this content. This in its turn suggests that someone voicing a T-comment attributing truth to Λ endorses the tenet that it is in fact possible that certain linguistic items express a truth and fail to do so at the same time.

Analogous consequences can be ascertained with respect to Σ in II). Regarding the situation considered in II*) the corresponding outcome is that, given the validity of (TE1), it is necessary for the truth of Ψ that

(α) Ψ expresses a truth
(β) Ω expresses a truth
(γ) Ψ fails to express a truth.

Deeply entrenched intuitions apparently militate against the supposition that those three conditions might be satisfied together. But if the validity of (TE2) were not acknowledged with respect to Ω, (α) could be still regarded as a requirement for the truth of Ψ, but the obligation to derive (α) from (β) or the untruth of (β) from (γ) would become otiose. This circumstance suggests that attributing lack of truth or failure of expressing a truth to Ψ does not necessarily lead to a contradiction. It involves an inconsistency merely in combination with either the assumption that Ψ actually expresses a truth or the supposition that (TE2) possesses unrestricted validity.

Our intuitive reluctance to attribute truth to either Λ, Σ or Ψ can be traced back to an easily comprehensible basis: The assumptions that

Λ, Σ or Ψ expresses a truth and that (a), (α) or an analogous proposition concerning Σ is true implies a contradiction which can be derived from the pertinent assumptions by bringing (TE1) but not (TE2) into play. This fact can be made conspicuous by invoking a derivation rule of '*self-entailment*' ('SE' for short) permitting to repeat any line of an argument, such that the repeated line depends on exactly the same assumptions as its predecessor. It implements the idea that every proposition entails itself. Logically, the rule is dispensable, of course, but in the present connection it serves the purpose of enhancing the transparency of our representation of paradox-ridden situations. Employing SE one can replace II) — and accordingly other pieces of reasoning — by the following derivational sequence:

(IIA)

1	(1)	Σ expresses that $\neg$ E Σ	A
2	(2)	E Σ	A
2	(3)	E Σ	2 SE
1,2	(4)	$\neg$ E Σ	1,3 EE
1,2	(5)	E Σ & $\neg$ E Σ	3,4 &I
1	(6)	$\neg$ E Σ	2,5 RAA

Thus, it becomes fully manifest that under certain circumstances an acknowledgment of (TE2) leads to consequences which blatantly contradict propositions which are derivable by employing most plausible principles — provided the property of being highly plausible is acknowledged not only with respect to the idea that every proposition entails itself but also regarding (TE1) and the corresponding rule 'EE'. By admitting the validity of 'SE' and 'EE' and admitting in addition that propositions which make contradictions derivable can never be true one is compelled to recognize that it must be impossible that items like Σ express anything true. This evidently raises the problem of explaining why it ought to be impossible to attribute (expressing a) truth to the concerned units despite the fact that apparently the content which they express is not contradictory or inconsistent.

The subsequent attempt at an explanation proceeds in two steps.

(1) In the light of the previous observation that the truth of Π requires that the conditions specified in both (a) and (b) are fulfilled it appears imperative to suppose that the truth of a T-comment ascribing truth to that item requires, apart from the circumstance that it expresses a truth itself, first, that Π in fact expresses a truth and second, that in fact Napoleon Bonaparte made war on Prussia. Hence a full explication of the necessary requirements of expressing a truth on the part of a T-comment ascribing truth to Π would involve more than that which the comment explicitly expresses — namely the fact that Π expresses a truth — even if one leaves out of account the requirement that it expresses a truth itself. Against this backdrop we can differentiate between two sorts of content which might be labelled (i) '*linguistic(ally conveyed) content*' and (ii) '*holistic content*'. With regard to Π, the first type of content would correspond to the proposition that Π expresses a truth whereas the holistic content consists in the conjunction of the propositions that Π expresses a truth and that Napoleon Bonaparte made war on Prussia, i.e. all the relevant truth-requirements except the condition that the comment itself expresses a truth. The difference between these two varieties of content can be generalized and applied to all kinds of T-comment. It would be natural to identify the holistic content of a T-comment denying truth with respect to Π with the conjunction of the propositions that Π expresses a truth and that it is not the case that Napoleon Bonaparte made war on Prussia, so the truth denial would entail the falsity of the content that is (linguistically) expressed by the item that functions as an object of comment. But it is important to note that the situation need not always be like this: Generally speaking, a truth denial claims merely that *not all conditions which would be required for something's being true are satisfied*. Therefore a truth disclaimer could be rendered true either by the circumstance that some unit functioning as an object of comment does not possess any intelligible meaning permitting to associate the item with a definite content or by the fact that the item lacks any content which is capable of being true or untrue or by the untruth of some relevant content that need not be equivalent to the content which the object of comment linguistically expresses.

(2) The combination of (TE1) and (TE2) amounts to the same as a principle which can be expressed by the formulation

> (TE*) [For any linguistic unit s:] If s expresses that p, then s (thereby) expresses a truth *if and only if* p.

It can be gathered from this formulation that the combination of (TE1) and (TE2) implies some specification regarding the pertinent meaning of the word 'express'. If the validity of (TE*) is acknowledged, it follows that the verb 'express' is to be employed in such a manner that whenever some item expresses something or other it must hold good that the item expresses a truth (in the pertinent sense of the term 'express') if and only if that which it expresses is the case. Considered in isolation the above specified theorem could be regarded as a mere stipulation which could compete with alternative stipulations, in particular with one implied by a principle that reads

> (TE1*) [For any linguistic unit s:] If s expresses that p, then s (thereby) expresses a truth *only if* p.

It is not difficult to discern that the alternative represented by (TE1*) is induced by the supposition that (TE1), but not (TE2) possesses unrestricted validity. But it seems that a propensity to admit the validity of (TE*) is widely shared, hence a disposition to employ the terms 'express' and particularly 'express a truth' — or similar terms — in a sense that complies with that principle should be quite common. This disposition is clearly discernible in pieces of reasoning alluded to before which argue that if an item claiming its own untruth were in fact untrue, it would follow that it expresses a truth and is true — because, allegedly, things would stand exactly as the item says they stand.

As a matter of fact, one can reasonably dispute the proposition that if sentences disclaiming truth regarding themselves fail to be true it inevitably follows that things stand exactly as those sentences say they stand. If the import of the truth denials articulated in Λ and Σ conforms with (TE*) then, according to an important and natural sense of 'say', they do not say everything which is relevant for their expressing something true. The formulation of a T-comment ascribing the quality of (expressing a) truth to Π typically does not reveal that (if it expresses a truth then) it is a truth that Napoleon Bonaparte has made war on Prussia, in other words, that Π expresses a truth *by expressing that Napoleon Bonaparte made war on Prussia.* A truth denial formulated by

> Π is not true / Π does not express a truth / What Π expresses is not a truth.

does not 'say' in the envisaged sense of the word, that (if the comment is true then) Π cannot express something true *on account of the fact that it expresses that Napoleon Bonaparte made war on Prussia*. In the same way Λ and Σ do not explicitly convey that (if they were true then) they cannot express a truth by expressing that they do not express anything true. Specifically under the considered assumption concerning the import of the term 'express', they do not (explicitly) say that their expressing something true does not only require that they fail to express a truth but also that the proposition that they fail to express a truth is not a truth. What they explicitly convey represents merely a necessary condition but not a condition that is both necessary and sufficient for their (expressing a) truth. A full specification of their relevant truth requirements is only provided by the *holistic* content which is the conjunction of the propositions that the concerned sentences do not express a truth and that it is not a truth that those sentences do not express a truth. Similarly, if the denial expressed by Ω in II*) conforms with (TE*), then the item fails to say, in the pertinent sense of this word, that the proposition that Ω expresses a truth is not true. Accordingly, the *holistic* import of Ω is to be identified with the contention that Ψ fails to express a truth *and* that it is not true that it itself, i.e. Ω, expresses something true.

On the other hand, the consequences would palpably differ, if the truth disclaimers were to possess an import that is not in conformity with (TE*) but rather with (TE1*). If their import were to comply with (TE1*) the supposition that Λ or Σ fail to be true would not license the derivation of the consequence that it is not the case that the pertinent items fail to express a truth. The relevant supposition would merely amount to the claim that it is not the case that all the requirements for expressing a truth on the part of Λ or Σ are met, hence there would be no commitment to the effect that lack of truth is due to the untruth of the explicitly conveyed content. As regards Ω in II*), its truth-denial regarding Ψ would imply that it cannot be the case that all necessary truth requirements regarding Ψ are satisfied; but there would be no (strict) entailment to the effect that the truth ascription expressed in Ψ is an untruth. The variant conceptions of being related to a content correlate with differences of holistic import. Truth denials which are in accordance with (TE*) represent stronger claims than truth denials complying with (TE1*). Accordingly, as far as the items considered above are concerned, truth paradoxes are generated exclusively on the basis of concepts of content-expression that accord with (TE*).

Although linguistically conveyed and holistic contents of T-comments generally differ, they often, and presumably in a vast majority of cases, correlate with equivalent propositions. If a T-comment attributes truth to Π it will express a truth not only if and only if Π in fact expresses a truth, but also if and only if it is a fact that Napoleon Bonaparte made war on Prussia. Similarly, a denial of truth regarding Π ought to express a truth precisely if Π fails to express a truth and if it is not a truth that Napoleon Bonaparte made war on Prussia. This circumstance could explain the existence of an entrenched disposition to conceive the word 'express' or similar terms connecting linguistic units with contents as being in accordance with (TE*) and thus to interpret truth denials as implying negations of a content explicitly conveyed by the commented item(s). But the fact that cases exist where the equivalence does not hold good does not only demand a differentiation between the two varieties of import but also calls for a terminological distinction between corresponding types of relations connecting linguistic items with content. In this vein let us introduce a terminological distinction between '*linguistically express*' or simply '*express*' for relations between expressions and linguistic contents and '*holistically express*' or '*express**' for relations between expressions and holistic contents. A parallel difference pertaining to the notion of meaning can be signalled by terminologically distinguishing between '*mean*' and '*mean**'. With respect to T-comments 'mean' serves to signify a relation between a T-comment and an import induced by its linguistic meaning, while 'mean*' is employed to signify a relation between a T-comment and *all* the relevant requirements for its (expressing a) truth. In accordance with these stipulations, one is entitled to assert that a T-comment characterising Π as a sentence that expresses a truth means that Π is a sentence that expresses a truth and means* that Π is a sentence that expresses a truth and that Napoleon Bonaparte made war on Prussia. Generally, a sentence of the form 'X means* that p' can be paraphrased by formulations such as 'X's being true/expressing a truth means that p' or 'that X is true/expresses a truth means that p'. Against this background it becomes patent that strictly speaking the relationship signalled by 'mean*' does not directly pertain to linguistic items and to propositional contents but rather to qualities or facts pertaining to linguistic items on the one hand and to propositions on the other. Even T-comments generating truth paradoxes do not refute the contention that those propositions are qualified for the status of bearers of absolute truth.

Only holistic contents can provide exhaustive and explicit specifications of conditions relevant for the truth of T-comments. Provided that holistic contents amount to conditions that are not only necessary but also sufficient for truth, the relational concept signified by 'express*' complies with (TE*). If the existence of the circumstance that (it is the case that) p is necessary and sufficient for the existence of the circumstance that some item S expresses a truth so that it holds good that

> S expresses a truth if and only if (it is the case that) p.

then the principle

> [For any linguistic unit s:] If s expresses* that p, then s (thereby) expresses* a truth if and only if p.

ought to be generally valid under the proviso that the holistic contents which constitute the range of the relation of expressing* provide necessary and sufficient conditions of truth for items in the domain.

Hence it would be totally inappropriate to dismiss (TE*) and (TE2) as invalid. Instead one needs to add a qualification to the effect that they are valid *with respect to holistic contents*, but not, at least not generally, with respect to contents linguistically conveyed in T-comments. The root of the paradoxes of truth considered so far lies in the circumstance that the principles (TE*) and (TE2) are associated with inappropriate types of content. The prejudice that a failure to express a truth on the part of a negative T-comment must be due to the untruth of the explicitly conveyed content of its object of comment is apt to induce the disconcerting consequence that the pertinent T-comment can neither be assessed as true nor as failing to be true. The urge to accept this consequence vanishes if the pertinent presupposition is dropped by acknowledging the possibility that truth-failure of a T-comment can result from the untruth of its holistic content which alone represents its necessary and sufficient conditions of truth, conditions that are not fully manifested by its formulation.

Against the background of the different varieties of content as well as different concepts of expressing a content it is not difficult to explain how one can consistently attribute absence of truth or failure of expressing a truth to the items Λ, Σ and Ψ in I), II) and II*). One (presumably) asserts something true if one contends that those items do not express* something that is true because, if the concepts of expressing referred to in those sentences comply with (TE*) they entail — in a way that does not depend on the validity of (TE*) — that the concerned units both fail to express something true and do not fail to express something true. Provided one accepts that contradictions cannot be true and that assumptions entailing contradictions cannot be true either, one is obliged to admit that everybody who expresses a denial of the truth of the holistic contents connected with Λ, Σ and Ψ thereby asserts a truth. The crucial reason lies in the circumstance that somebody who disclaims the truth of the pertinent holistic contents makes a different and weaker claim than anybody who claims in addition that the failure of expressing a truth on the part of the relevant items must be due to the untruth of their linguistically conveyed imports. The upshot is that the holistic contents of T-comments commenting on T-comments can differ in accordance with different conceptions of expressing a content, even if the difference need not (always) be manifested on the linguistic level. This is the case if a terminology is employed which does not reflect the distinction between 'express' and 'express*' as explained above. In this manner differences of truth value correlate with differences of (holistic) content.

A most important consequence of the account delineated in this section is that assessing matters of truth and specifying conditions of expressing truth essentially transcend the framework of linguistic or philological investigations. They require, at least from a theoretical perspective, to bring a concept of meaning into play which differs from the conception of meaning that stands in the focus within linguistics and traditional philology. If this phenomenon were restricted to the realm of few specimens of truth denials it might be dismissed as practically irrelevant. So, the circumstance that paradoxes of truth are not confined to T-comments expressing or implying truth denials regarding themselves possesses significance.

IV. Applications of the Theory

Although (TE2) plays a pivotal role for the derivation of paradoxes a rejection of (TE2) by itself falls short of providing satisfactory answers to various questions our attempt to (dis)solve truth paradoxes is likely to provoke. The following (nine) applications of that account are meant to shed more light on the nature of that account by addressing worries which may still persist.

(1)

One might find it puzzling that a restriction of validity should be imposed on (TE2) which does not affect in the same manner (TE1). According to the account delineated above (TE1) is even applicable to kinds of content which are explicitly conveyed by linguistic units for deriving consequences from the assumption that they express a truth. Does this amount to an undue prejudice favouring (TE1) over (TE*) and (TE2)? As a matter of fact, the adopted position does not involve any unjustified partiality. (TE2) clearly represents a potentially stronger claim than (TE1), and this potential becomes specifically significant in the realm of T-comments. The reason why (TE2) involves a stronger claim than (TE1) lies in the circumstance that a statement to the effect that

If (it is the case that) p then s by expressing that p expresses a truth.

is potentially more vulnerable than

If s by expressing that p expresses a truth, then (it is the case that) p.

If the condition that a sentence expresses a truth comprises among others the truth of the (propositional) content which is explicitly expressed by it, then the pertinent condition, i.e. the sentence's expressing a truth, is potentially stronger than the truth of the explicitly expressed proposition; the former entails the latter, but not necessarily vice versa. In (TE1) the stronger requirement appears in the antecedent and the weaker in the consequent clause, whereas in (TE2), the other way around, the weaker in the antecedent and the stronger in the consequent clause.[30] Hence, other things being equal, a satisfaction of (TE1) guarantees a satisfaction of (TE2), but not necessarily vice versa. To be sure, in cases such as Π truth of the explicitly expressed content constitutes both a necessary and a sufficient condition of the truth of the item expressing that content.[31] But as soon as one takes T-comments into account the situation fundamentally changes. The reason is that T-comments can, and usually, do involve an implicit (!) comment pertaining to the content(s) linguistically conveyed by the items functioning as their objects of comment and that its correctness constitutes a necessary requirement for the T-comment's (expressing a) truth.[32]

---

[30] The circumstances that (TE2) is equivalent to the principle that, if a linguistic item expressing that p fails to express a truth then (it is) not (true that) p, puts into relief a crucial aspect of its vulnerability: If it were universally valid, untruth of expressed content would be the only possible reason for failure of expressing a truth. However, in I) and other specimens of derivation the consequence of failure of expressing a truth is not based on the untruth of the expressed content of a pertinent unit but on the fact that the supposition of its expressing a truth leads to an inconsistency (if TE1 is not repudiated).

[31] Considering (unequivocal) linguistic items containing indexical constituents one ought to say more precisely: The truth of the proposition determined by the explicitly expressed linguistic meaning in combination with pertinent contextual features constitutes a necessary *and* sufficient condition for the sentence's expressing a truth.

[32] The property of implicitly taking a position on contents associated with (other) items is not confined to the area of T-comments. If a speaker A were to utter assertively the

Nothing which is (or has been) asserted by me has ever been asserted by B.

the assertion can only be true — given that the universal quantification is not restricted — if, in fact, B has never asserted that nothing asserted by A has ever been asserted by him, and if it should happen that both A and B have once asserted that the earth is round, the pertinent assertion cannot be true (at least according to one reading of the sentence).

(2)

The last contention is compatible with the fact that T-comments do not always imply substantial verdicts about the content of their objects, a fact which comes to light if one considers examples like

> Napoleon Bonaparte was an orthodox Hindu. That sentence either expresses a truth or fails to do so.

But examples like the one considered in V) indicate that also in the realm of complex T-comments implicit comments on qualities of objects of comment are by no means generally irrelevant. A major reason lies in the circumstance that (natural) languages permit the coinage of linguistic units which exhibit the peculiarity that their lack of truth warrants the truth of their explicitly expressed content. In order to cast more light on the pertinent matter it appears suitable to consider an informal piece of reasoning based on a modification of the example considered in V). It exhibits an immediate instead of an indirect self-reference and is reminiscent of the so-called 'Curry-paradox' — or 'Löb's paradox'. Let us suppose that some speaker U utters

> (Z) If the sentence which I am uttering just now expresses a truth then Napoleon Bonaparte was an orthodox Hindu.

one could reason as follows:

VIII)

(1) Suppose that the sentence (Z) uttered by U expresses a truth.

(2) Then (it is true that) if the sentence (Z) uttered by U expresses a truth then Napoleon Bonaparte was an orthodox Hindu [in accordance with (TE1)].

(3) Consequently, it holds true that if the sentence (Z) uttered by U expresses a truth then Napoleon Bonaparte was an orthodox Hindu [as this conclusion is vindicated by the rule of Conditional Proof it does not depend on the original assumption].

(4) But (Z) expresses (in the supposed context) exactly this, namely that if the sentence (Z) uttered by U expresses a truth then Napoleon Bonaparte was an orthodox Hindu.

(5) Consequently, the sentence (Z) uttered by U expresses a truth [in accordance with (TE2)].

(6) Ergo: Napoleon Bonaparte was an orthodox Hindu [by *modus ponendo ponens* from 3 and 5].

If this piece of reasoning were impeccable, cases would exist where an utterance of a linguistic item of the form 'If A then B' validates the conclusion that the antecedent of the conditional expresses a truth, where the truth of this conclusion does not depend on the assumption that the antecedent expresses in fact a truth. But the derivation of line (5) from (4) is not possible if (TE2) does not automatically license the conclusion that an item can be considered as being true or as expressing a truth given that its explicitly expressed content represents a truth and if one insists that (TE2) can be applied only if the complete set of conditions of being true, which comprise, among others, the (a)-component, viz. that the concerned item is in fact true or expresses a truth, is fulfilled. If (TE2) can be applied only under the more restricted conditions [33] the conclusion of line (6) could not be vindicated by the circumstance alone that (it is true that) if the sentence (Z) uttered by U expresses a truth then Napoleon Bonaparte was an orthodox Hindu but only by this circumstance *in combination with* the supposition that the sentence (Z) uttered by U actually expresses a truth. This means that the assumption formulated in the first line constitutes an indispensable factor for the truth of the proposition expressed in line (6). Thus at least in the realm of T-comments the assumption that its (a)-component holds true can constitute a substan-

[33] This means that (TE2) is applicable with respect to the content which is explicitly expressed by the sentence: 'The sentence (Z) uttered by U expresses a truth and if the sentence (Z) uttered by U expresses a truth then Napoleon Bonaparte was an orthodox Hindu.'

tial addition to the supposition that its (b)-component, viz. its explicitly formulated content, is a truth. In the case of (Z) lack of truth of the (a)-component should guarantee the truth of the (b)-component, given that a (material) conditional 'If A then B' expresses a truth whenever the antecedent clause fails to express a truth. Seen in this light the thesis that truth of the (b)-component cannot by itself guarantee the truth of the (a)-component and that accordingly the supposition of the truth of the latter can constitute a substantial addition to the supposition of the truth of the former harmonizes with a pre-theoretic intuition.

Since

(i) the application of (TE2) — in combination with (TE1) — to an explicitly expressed content has the effect that its truth must constitute not only a necessary but also a sufficient condition for the ascription of (the property of expressing a) truth to an item expressing it, and

(ii) with respect to specific T-comments, such as (Z), the requirements for truth ascriptions are thereby relaxed in a way that even lack of truth licenses them,

propositions are derivable which could otherwise not be derived. In the case of examples like (Z) the crucial factor lies in the derivability of a proposition which occurs as an antecedent in an equally derivable conditional creating the condition for the applicability of the rule of *modus ponendo ponens*. It emerges as a result that expressing a truth on the part of (Z) would require the truth of the proposition that Napoleon Bonaparte was an orthodox Hindu, whereas this is not necessary for the truth of the explicitly expressed propositional content.

Quite similar observations can be made regarding pieces of reasoning which start from assumptions concerning the co-referentiality of different linguistic items. In this connection certain fallacies based on inappropriate basic assumptions have to be forestalled. In particular formulations of the forms

(i) A = 'A → B'
(ii) A = (A → B)
(iii) A ↔ (A → B) or: A if and only if (A → B)

are unsuitable. The first two have to be avoided on account of syntactic and semantic incongruities: The identity symbol '=' requires that the symbol 'A' at its left represents a singular term, whereas the occurrence of the same symbol at the left of '→' requires that it represents a sentence.[34] (iii) is syntactically well-formed but represents an invalid formula, which becomes obvious if one replaces 'A' by a truth and 'B' by an untruth; it had been laid down, however, that the term 'truth paradox' ought to be applied only in situations where (apparently) inacceptable conclusions are derivable from *prima facie* plausible assumptions. The reason for mentioning those facts lies in the circumstance that they seem to be unduly disregarded now and then.[35]

In contrast the following formulation

(iv) A = 'E A →B'

where 'E' is to be interpreted as before, is acceptable and can serve as a basis for the following argument:

IX)

1	(1)	A = 'E A →B'[36]	A
2	(2)	E A	A
1,2	(3)	E 'E A →B'	On account of identity-assumption in (1)
1,2	(4)	E A →B	Based on (TE1)
1,2	(5)	B	2,4 MPP
1	(6)	E A →B	2,5 CP

[34] In order to avoid unneeded complications it is preferable not to present the matter in a way which suggests the disputable Fregean conception of sentences as names (of truth values).

[35] Cf. In this connection the expositions of Curry's paradox in the 'Wikipedia' or Bocheński/Menne 1973:92–93.

[36] Obviously, in this formula 'A' is a placeholder for singular terms, while 'B' is a placeholder for sentences.

1	(7) E 'E A →B'	Based on (TE2)
1	(8) E A	On account of identity-assumption in (1)
1	(9) B	6,8 MPP

According to (TE2), if something is the case then anything which expresses that this is the case expresses a truth. Here again this principle is exploited for deriving some arbitrary conclusion. It turns out that the truth of B is a necessary requirement for accrediting truth to A — which is clearly manifested by line (5), as it depends (apart from the assumption of the first line) on line (2) — although it is not necessary for the truth of the explicitly expressed content of the sentence designated by A.

The situation envisaged in IX) represents a realistic possibility. One can, for example, specify contextual features to an extent that only one linguistic item is produced in a particular context. Given that 'C' signifies such a unique context of utterance and that in C the sentence

> If the (only) sentence uttered in C expresses a truth, then Napoleon Bonaparte was an orthodox Hindu.

is uttered: Then the expressions 'the (only) sentence uttered in C' and "If the (only) sentence uttered in C expresses a truth, then Napoleon Bonaparte was an orthodox Hindu" denote the same linguistic item (token or type), so that

> the (only) sentence uttered in C = 'if the (only) sentence uttered in C expresses a truth, then Napoleon Bonaparte was an orthodox Hindu.'

can be assumed.

(3)

The circumstance that in all these cases a T-comment's being true definitely relies on additional factors apart from the truth of its explicit content, inasmuch as its truth (indirectly) depends on the content and truth values of items which function as objects of comment, furnishes additional support for disputing the general validity of (TE2). At this point one has to face the following objection: The claim that the advocated thesis harmonizes with common intuitions can hardly be maintained. For isn't it plain that a T-comment expresses something true whenever that which it explicitly expresses is true? Here one has to take into account an equivocation inhering in expressions, such as 'express a truth', 'express something which is true', which is not considered in the previously highlighted distinction between different readings of those phrases coping with the problem that items functioning as objects of T-comments can be ambiguous. If one considers a complex sentence like

> Managua is the capital of Nicaragua and Napoleon Bonaparte was born in Austria.

in some sense it would be legitimate to say that the pertinent item expresses a truth or something which is true. The reason lies evidently in the fact that the first component of the conjunction is, or expresses, a truth. But it is equally legitimate, of course, to deny ascription of truth to the complex expression because one conjunct is not true. For the time being it is not necessary to dispute the contention that in the former and weaker sense of the phrase 'express a truth' even T-comments like Λ, Σ, Ψ, Ω, Γ, Δ etc. might express something which is true. In any case, ascriptions of truth to T-comments should be orientated by the principle that the truth of all conjuncts in a conjunction is required for ascriptions of truth to a conjunction as a whole. There is no need to embark on discussions about the question which of the variant interpretations harmonizes better with common linguistic intuitions. What matters in the present connection is rather the following: 1) The proposed interpretation must not militate against common linguistic practice, 2) it must be clear and intelligible, 3) it ought to yield theoretical benefits, 4) it should not be favoured only for the sake of allowing for some *ad hoc* solution of theoretical problems, 5) the views built on this stance ought to possess a considerable degree of plausibility even if one disregards the fact that truth paradoxes exist.

(4)

It could be preferable to abstain from the employment of the term ‘express’ for signalling a relation between meaningful linguistic items and something that transcends their explicitly represented content. The previously considered terminological distinctions between ‘express’ and ‘express*’ as well as between ‘mean’ and ‘mean*’ embody a possible way of overcoming relevant defects. Against this background one could with respect to formulations representing T-comments in a less explicit manner employ the ideas of being true or being untrue (failing to be true) *under an interpretation*. Expressions like ‘S expresses a truth’, ‘S fails to express a truth’ exhibit by themselves a particular sort of vagueness resulting from the circumstance that the ordinary term ‘express’ is underdetermined: It can be explicated in a way that it (exclusively) concerns the explicitly expressed linguistic contents of units which function as object(s) of comment; but it can be equally explicated as a relation between linguistic items and ‘holistic’ contents that are not fully manifested by their linguistic import. Consequently, it can occur that T-comments are alternatively classifiable as being true, i.e. as expressing a truth, or as untrue, i.e. as failing to express a truth, in accordance with the way in which they are interpreted and explicated. This phenomenon will now be elucidated in more detail.

The linguistic content of (Z), for example, viz.

> If the sentence which I am uttering just now expresses a truth then Napoleon Bonaparte was an orthodox Hindu.

consists in the conditional that if the sentence (Z) uttered by U expresses a truth then Napoleon Bonaparte was an orthodox Hindu, whereas its holistic counterpart encompasses the conjunction of the linguistic content together with the proposition that Napoleon Bonaparte was an orthodox Hindu.[37] This shows how substantial the

---

[37] The explication

> If the sentence which I am uttering just now expresses a truth then Napoleon Bonaparte was an orthodox Hindu, and if that is a truth — i.e. if it holds good that if the sentence which I am uttering just now expresses a truth then

disparity between the two content-types can become. But it is a common phenomenon that truth-value ascriptions do not explicitly indicate a contrast between different types of content. To be sure, regarding sentences of the form 'It is (not) true that p' as for instance

> (S1) It is (not) true that Napoleon Bonaparte was an orthodox Hindu.

it holds usually good that the truth of their explicitly expressed content constitutes a necessary as well as a sufficient condition for their expressing a truth. But truth-assessments of T-comments, such as

> (S2) That is (not) true.

require first an explication which specifies the contextually induced or intended reference of the deictic expression, which could be provided by, say:

> (S2*) That, namely (the proposition) that Napoleon Bonaparte was an orthodox Hindu, is (not) true.

In such cases one might distinguish between (i) a linguistically expressed content in the strict sense and (ii) a propositional content induced by the linguistic content. Considering examples, such as:

> (S3) If what our president has said is true, then two plus two equals ten million.

one can equally ascertain that evaluating truth or lack of truth can only be accomplished if what was said by the contextually pertinent president is specified, as, for example, in the following explication:

> Napoleon Bonaparte was an orthodox Hindu — then Napoleon Bonaparte was an orthodox Hindu.

exhibiting the form of 'If p then q, and if (if p then q) then q' which equivalent with 'If p then q, and q' reveals this fact.

(S3*) If (what our president has said, namely) that the situation in our country is better than ever before is true, then two plus two equals ten million.[38]

Here one could argue that the truth of the explicitly expressed content need not matter for the question of whether one ought to agree or disagree with the statement. Agreement or disagreement need not be affected by the issue of whether it was in fact *said* by a president that the situation in some particular country is better than ever before. Decisive importance might be rather attributed to the question of whether or not it is really the case that the situation in the pertinent country is better than ever before. But this presumably only shows that one needs to differentiate between the question of a T-comment's expressing a truth on the one hand and the legitimacy of attributing truth to the utterance made by its employment on the other. Moreover, it is easy to see that apart from a literally expressed content both (S3) and (S3*) suggest an implicature to the effect that it is completely absurd to suppose that the situation (at some particular time) in some country is better than ever before. It emerges that apart from linguistic and holistic contents also other types of contents can function as a basis for truth assessments concerning T-comments.

The possibility of substantial divergences between linguistic and holistic contents arises because T-comments typically possess implications pertaining to truth or absence of truth of contents that are not specified by their literal import. This can happen, as in the examples (S2) and (S3), because a T-comment, although referring to some content, does not present a specification of the content to which it refers. Similarly as in the case of deictic expressions or definite descriptions like 'The favourite colour of Hans Dietrich Genscher' where one can appropriately ask 'But what is the favourite colour of Hans Dietrich Genscher?' one can ask analogous questions with respect to (S2) and (S3): 'But what is that which is allegedly true or

[38] A well-grounded judgment about truth or lack of truth would require further specifications as regards the reference of 'our country' and as regards the time which functions as the implicit relatum of the word 'before'.

not true?', 'What is that which the president said?'. The same predicament occurs if a T-comment does not contain elements purporting to refer to any content at all. Most pertinent examples are items referring to linguistic units, specifically individual sentences, as well as T-comments exhibiting quantifications, such as

(S4) The last sentence on page four does not express a truth.
(S5) All sentences expressing universal propositions are untrue.
(S6) All assertions Nancy made about Napoleon are untenable.
(S7) Nothing true is ever said on this spot.

They all imply consequences pertaining to the possession or lack of truth of possible propositional contents that are not specified by them.[39] In this regard it does not matter whether they refer to linguistic or non-linguistic entities or whether they do not refer to individual objects at all. Since sentences referring to linguistic objects share with other sorts of T-comments the highlighted crucial feature, focussing for the sake of illustration on cases which exhibit reference to linguistic items does not distort the account. A basis for differentiating between different types of content, and in particular between linguistic and holistic content, can be detected even if one disregards truth paradoxes.

The truth of a negative T-comment, i.e. of a truth denial, which claims that not all necessary requirements for (expressing a) truth are fulfilled, depends on various factors. This idea appears most natural against the background of the existence of a larger plurality of contents. One can in fact establish that there are several possibilities, such as 1) meaninglessness of items functioning as objects of T-comments, 2) non-existence of (propositional) content, e.g. in the case

[39] Even with respect to sentences implying truth denials regarding their own linguistic content like

The sentence which I am uttering just now does not express any truth at all.

one can ascertain that the implication about their own content, viz. that it is not a truth that the sentence the speaker is uttering does not express a truth at all, is not, and cannot be, (linguistically) expressed by the sentence the speaker is uttering.

of interjections, which can be credited with meaning but not with a content assessable as true or untrue, 3) untruth of some literally expressed content, 4) untruth of a propositional content induced by literal meaning in combination with features of context, if linguistic tokens are at stake, 5) untruth of some holistic content, 6) untruth of implicatures induced by 'conversational maxims'. In the present connection the varieties 3)–5) possess primary importance. The circumstance that those differences are not signalled by common formulations must not mislead one into supposing that they are irrelevant. On the contrary, this fact is suited to highlight the significance of explications.

(5)

In section III above it was shown by argument II.A) that an item Σ that supposedly expresses that it does not express something true entails a contradiction, given (i) that all instances of 'P → P' are true and that the corresponding derivation rule of 'self-entailment' is valid and (ii) that (TE1) holds true and the corresponding derivation rule 'EE' is valid. It was suggested that this fact should motivate us to reject any supposition to the effect that Σ expresses a truth. Now this might appear counterintuitive for the following reason: Assuming it is in fact true that Σ fails to express a truth and that Σ linguistically expresses that Σ fails to express a truth; should one not admit that that which Σ linguistically expresses is a truth and that accordingly there must be something true which Σ linguistically expresses? Should we not reject the supposition that Σ's entailing a contradiction provides a solid basis for denying Σ's truth? Or should we admit in the end that Σ is both truc and untrue?

In the light of the foregoing observation the following reply might appear natural: The supposition that Σ is both true and fails to be true is merely apparently absurd; the two formulations 'Σ is true' and 'Σ fails to be true' only evoke the impression of incompatibility because they are not sufficiently explicit – which is due to the absence of any reference to a relation between linguistic items and content. Nevertheless, mere reference to a relation cannot provide a satisfying solution because the two formulations 'Σ expresses a truth' and 'Σ fails to express a truth' evoke the impression of incompatibility to the same degree. But it may appear that our distinction between 'express' and 'express*' offers a way-out. Could one not maintain that Σ expresses a truth and (at the same time) fails to express* a truth? It is important to recognize that and why this proposal cannot provide an appropriate answer to everything which matters in this area.

First, it cannot be taken for granted that the item designated by 'Σ' (linguistically) expresses a definite content capable of being categorically true. In the previous discussion the concept of expression that is a constituent of the import of Σ was not definitely fixed. This leaves room for the possibility that the pertinent notion of content expression is vague, being indeterminate between the alternatives of linguistically or holistically expressing. If, however, the tenet that Σ expresses a truth and fails to express* a truth were in fact correct it would be illegitimate to suppose that the circumstance that it linguistically expresses a truth could categorically bestow truth on the item, precisely because of the indeterminacy of its import. One could at most claim that in the current circumstances the item can be assessed as true on one explicatory reading and as failing to be true on another reading.

Second, and this is presumably more important, even on the supposition that the terminological framework in which Σ is embedded exhibits a degree of elaborateness that is (at least) as high as the one in which its assessment is embedded and that it refers to a definite concept of linguistic expression, the contention that 'there must be something true which Σ linguistically expresses' is less plausible than it initially appears. The structure of the linguistic import, as it has been conceived, can be explicated by the formulation

> For every x: If x is a content linguistically expressed by Σ then x is not a truth.

Now let us suppose that it is really the case that there is something true which Σ linguistically expresses. Then, given that no restriction is imposed on the universal quantification, the content of Σ patently militates against the pertinent supposition. Σ entails that if anything is a truth then this truth cannot be expressed by it. Thus, Σ denies the applicability of (TE2) to itself. Let 'c' stand for 'nothing which Σ linguistically expresses is a truth/is true'. Then the formulation

> For every x: If x is a content linguistically expressed by Σ, then x is not a truth, and if Σ linguistically expresses (the content) that c, then (the content) that c is not a truth/is not true.

yields an explication of the character of the pertinent universal quantification. In accordance with the principle 'p → q ⊢ (p & r) → q' the second conjunct, viz. 'and if ....', implies

> If Σ linguistically expresses (the content) that c and it is true that c, then (the content) that c is not a truth which is linguistically expressed by Σ, i.e. Σ does not express a truth by linguistically expressing that nothing which Σ linguistically expresses is a truth.

It becomes apparent that and why one can consistently maintain (i) that it is a truth or a fact that Σ does not express any truth and that this fact can be asserted in principle and (ii) that this truth cannot be expressed as a truth by Σ itself. The reason why one can truthfully assert the proposition that Σ does not linguistically express any truth by means of a different linguistic item, namely 'Nothing which Σ linguistically expresses is a truth', lies in the circumstance that by using that formulation one does not in the same manner counteract the truth of what is linguistically expressed and that one does not (implicitly) dispute the applicability of (TE2) to that content. It is Σ's way of implicitly counteracting which is apt to bestow truth on a T-comment denying Σ's truth.[40]

Obviously, a linguistic item's possessing a content does not imply its possessing a content that is capable of being assessed as true. To be sure, the manner in which Σ has been introduced assures us that the

---

[40] One might compare this with a situation where somebody utters

> It is true that Napoleon Bonaparte made war on Prussia, and when(ever) I say that Napoleon Bonaparte made war on Prussia I do not say anything true.

item designated by 'Σ' is a meaningful unit and on that account it should be credited with the quality of expressing something or other. It is, nonetheless, easy to ascertain that in this sense of expressing or possessing a content many linguistic items which in virtue of their meaning alone are not related to propositional contents exhibit this property. Examples are

— The first Nobel Prize laureate in physics
— is a Nobel Prize laureate
— Since W. C. Röntgen is the first Nobel Prize laureate in physics
— W. C. Röntgen is the first Nobel Prize laureate in physics and

The decisive point is that even from the circumstance that some unit belongs to the category of meaningful and complete declarative sentences it cannot be deduced that the pertinent item expresses a propositional content capable of being assessed as true, given that certain states of affairs obtain.[41] The suspicion that Σ belongs to a category of (linguistically impeccable) sentences whose content is not assessable as true is fuelled by the consideration that its content is specified on the basis of the notion of its own (expressed) content. As soon as one raises the question:

> What is (the content) expressed by Σ?

and finds oneself confronted with the answer:

> The content expressed by Σ is that Σ does not express anything which is true.

[41] Thus, from the assumption that Σ does not express any truth (whatsoever) one cannot derive, by the rule of universal quantifier elimination (or universal instantiation or specification) the conclusion that it is not a truth that Σ does not express any truth — and by the rules of '&'-introduction and *reductio ad absurdum* that Σ must express some truth. It can be only legitimate to infer that the content that Σ does not express any truth is not a truth which is expressed by Σ, i.e. that it is not both expressed by Σ and a truth. Only at this point the ordinary conception of expressing something — which orientates itself by linguistic items not involving self-reference or self-comment — requires an adjustment.

one is inevitably thrown back to the question:

What does it mean* that Σ does not express anything which is true?

and at this stage it appears to be impossible to specify any non-circular explanation of some condition which would be sufficient for vindicating its truth.[42] In this regard it does not matter, whether the term 'express' is to be explicated by 'linguistically express' or 'holistically express' or in some other way. Being confronted with the grammatically well-formed (English) sentence:

This is true.

one can easily discern (provided that one possesses the required linguistic competence and even supposing that a token of this sentence occurs as an example in a linguistic treatise) that it (the type or a token) expresses the same as

Das ist wahr.

in German or

Det är sant.

in Swedish etc. Here it is evident that knowing what something means does not automatically involve knowledge as to what something means*.

This observation is compatible with the fact that sometimes truth-conditions which are not question begging can be specified for items exhibiting this feature. Even disregarding questions of the interpretation of the letter 'A', 'B' or 'C' one can ascertain that, say,

$A \rightarrow B$

must represent a truth if 'B' is assessable as true or that

$(A \& B) \& C$

---

[42] The situation clearly contrasts with the state of affairs that can be ascertained, for example, regarding a truth denial concerning the item designated by 'N' in the context of V) in section II.D above.

can only be true if ‘C’ is assessable as true. For *this* question not only the issue regarding the values of ‘A’ and ‘B’ can be discounted but even the query of whether ‘C’ stands i) for an item whose content would be assessable as true given alternative circumstances or ii) for an entity that lacks any such content. On such a basis it is claimed that Σ needs to exhibit absence of truth, given that (TE1) and the impossibility of the truth of contradictions ought to be acknowledged.

Absence of linguistically expressed content capable of being assessed as true does not rule out the possession of a content which together with other contents is able to constitute some content that is definitely assessible with respect to truth or lack of truth. It is equally compatible with the suppositions that the (allegedly non-propositional) linguistic content of Σ can function as a target of (quasi-)reference and constitute an object of comment. This possibility is vindicated, e.g. by:

> Paul has won the first prize and this is something of which everybody can be proud.
>
> Eric is something which many politicians are and this is something of which one should be ashamed.

Here the occurrences of ‘this’ do not refer to objects like persons, events or propositions but substitute expressions like ‘winning the first prize’ and ‘to be something which many politicians are’.[43]

In this manner a difficulty is circumvented that emerges in a most conspicuous manner as soon as one considers a slightly modified wording of Σ which reads:

---

[43] From a technical point of view the imminent dilemma might be dissolved by stipulating that generally the linguistic contents of declarative sentences, even if they do not contain indexical constituents, are not propositions but functions of the type ‘P and .....’ so that such sentences express propositions only in combination with certain circumstantial conditions, such as the circumstance that a linguistic item does not imply a T-comment on itself or on its own content. — Note that line (2) in argument II) in section II or in argument II.A) in section III does not presuppose that Σ exhibits a content that is capable of being true. The introduction of this assumption merely conveys what would be true if the item were to possess a true content.

(Σ^+) What Σ^+ expresses is not true / is not a truth.

Let us hypothesize that the following identity holds good:

What Σ^+ expresses = the proposition that what Σ^+ expresses is not true / is not a truth.

Then the subsequent consequences have to be accepted:

What Σ^+ expresses is true if and only if the proposition that what Σ^+ expresses is not true is *true*.
What Σ^+ expresses is untrue if and only if the proposition that what Σ^+ expresses is not true is *untrue*.

After all, if

The first Nobel Prize laureate in physics = Wilhelm Conrad Röntgen

holds true it must be accepted as well that

The first Nobel Prize laureate in physics was born in Lennep if and only if Wilhelm Conrad Röntgen was born in Lennep.

etc. But if the identity hypothesized above is not maintained the disconcerting consequences do not result. The view that the expression 'what Σ^+ expresses' does not refer to any specific proposition is corroborated by the consideration that any attempt to specify the import of the item designated by it would in its turn involve a reference to the notion of being something which Σ^+ expresses.

The factor that bestows truth on the proposition that Σ fails to express a truth is a 'formal' circumstance, namely the fact that the supposition of its (expressing a) truth entails a contradiction and that it cannot be true that Σ, or any other linguistic item, fails to express a truth and at the same time does not fail to do so. It appears indeed incongruous to suppose that the factor which alone renders untrue the complex holistic content and imparts truth on its denial should equally bestow truth, or respectively untruth, to its elementary components.

One could say that only the holistic content represents a complete sense = thought.[44]

Given that the holistic content of Σ amounts to a contradiction[45] and assuming that not linguistic but holistic contents deserve to be treated as a basis for truth-value assignments — and that linguistic contents can play the same role only in a (admittedly) great number of cases where the different types of content do not materially differ — it follows that the pertinent item can be definitely assessed as being untrue or, more precisely, as failing to express any truth. Hence no ground exists for calling into question the validity of the rule of *reductio ad absurdum*. This mirrors the intuitive view that if someone would utter a sentence like

> (S7) The sentence which I am uttering just now does not express any truth at all.

he would commit himself, by assertively uttering this sentence, to acknowledge that any (linguistically) expressed content of his own sentence is not a truth and to admit that it is not a truth that the sentence uttered by him does not express any truth.

---

44 If a linguistic item L1 says about a linguistic item L2 that L2 does not express a truth, the content of L1 is incomplete in so far as its being true or untrue depends on what L2 means. If L1 says about L2 that L2 expresses a truth and fails to do so, then the question of L1's truth does not any more depend in the same manner on the meaning and sense of L2. Since the incompleteness characterises T-comments in general, it holds also good if L1 comments on itself, i.e. if L1 = L2.

45 A suitable paraphrase would read:

> Σ fails to express a truth and that, namely that Σ fails to express a truth, is not a truth/is not true.

Theoretically, this form of paraphrase could be even provided for 'ordinary' sentences, not implying any form of self-comment, for example:

> Napoleon Bonaparte made war on Prussia and that, namely that Bonaparte made war on Prussia, is a truth / is true.

for a sentence expressing that Napoleon Bonaparte made war on Prussia. The difference is that in ordinary cases paraphrases of this type do not provide additional information relevant for truth-value assessments.

At this point an objection ought to be forestalled which runs as follows: If Σ should fail to express a truth or can be definitely assessed as lacking the property of being true, then it should be possible to correctly assert that this is the case. Accordingly, it must be possible to express a truth by saying:

Σ fails to express a truth.

But if we are able to express a truth by ascribing absence of truth with respect to Σ, why should Σ fail to express anything true if it ascribes the same attribute to itself? Given that both Σ and some Σ' consist in the same chain of words employed in exactly the same sense, how could only one of them expresses a truth?

A partial response to this objection has been indicated before. In addition one should recall the fact that in the realm of items containing indexical elements linguistic synonymy generally does not go hand in hand with expression of contents possessing identical truth values. Specifically, regarding certain sentences with token-reflexive ingredients, such as

The sentence written here is a well-formed English sentence.

replacements by linguistically synonymous expressions of other languages are even bound to alter the truth value. By assuming that T-comments possessing identical linguistic import can differ with respect to truth value, a phenomenon observable in one realm is merely extended to another realm.

It is, however, also imperative to consider more precisely the question of what one in fact asserts about Σ if one truly asserts that Σ fails to express a truth. Evidently the verdict that Σ fails to express a truth was based on the consideration that its holistic content cannot be true, because both the requirements that the concerned item does not express any truth and that it is not the case that it does not express any truth cannot be satisfied together. But by claiming that Σ entails a contradiction and supposing that the conjunctive propositions

Σ expresses a truth and it is not the case that Σ expresses a truth.

> It is not true that Σ expresses a truth and it is not true that it is not true that Σ expresses a truth.

must fail to be true one does not pass a verdict on the truth or lack of truth of either conjunct. One neither disputes the truth of the proposition that Σ expresses a truth in particular nor the truth of the proposition that it is not true that Σ expresses a truth in particular. But the verdict to the effect that Σ fails to express a truth because its holistic content amounts to a contradiction which cannot be true rests on the assumption that Σ itself involves a truth denial with respect to its own linguistically expressed content. Hence the holistic contents of the two T-comments, i.e. Σ and the allegedly true verdict about Σ, markedly differ. In this manner the possibility of assigning different truth values can be traced back to a difference of (holistic) content, and the principle that one and the same (completely specified) proposition cannot possess several mutually exclusive truth values need not be violated. It holds true, however, that certain pairs of T-comments, such as Σ and one expressing a verdict about Σ, which can be used for stating different propositions deviating with respect to truth value, are linguistically synonymous. Hence it is, strictly speaking, not appropriate to say that Σ and the item conveying a verdict about Σ express different propositions; one ought rather to resort to a term like 'express*', as explicated above, for formulating the relevant fact. The upshot is that the use of a sentence exhibiting the reading of Σ does not make *mandatory* an interpretation according to which it involves a denial regarding its linguistically conveyed content.

According to the view propagated in the present essay the circumstance that one can assert a truth by using an item expressing that Σ fails to be true or to express anything true is apt to induce a delusion: the delusion that a content consisting in a truth denial regarding some linguistic item exhibits the quality of being true. In reality, however, contents (linguistically) expressed by T-comments ascribing or denying truth regarding linguistic expressions are themselves *never* capable of being categorically true. They cannot exhibit this property as long as they are not supplemented by some specification of a content which items functioning as their object(s) possess. This is, however, perfectly compatible with the fact that T-comments lacking explicit specifications in this respect can be employed for making true *assertions* pertaining to issues of truth regarding linguistic items against the background of contents which those items possess.[46] In this light one can discern an affinity between contents expressed by T-comments and contents linguistically conveyed by sentences containing indexical elements.

(6)

The phenomenon that linguistically synonymous items, even if they do not contain deictic ingredients, are able to alternatively convey different propositions potentially deviating with respect to truth value is by no means uncommon in the realm of T-comments. A most elementary instance is provided by T-comments on linguistically ambiguous items, such as

(S8) In every Swedish village there is more than one bank.

The truth value of a T-comment on a token of (S8) is crucially affected by the identity of the (linguistic) content of that token.

Similar situations can even occur if items functioning as objects of T-comments are free from linguistic ambiguities in the genuine sense of the term. A pertinent example is provided by sentences whose quantifications can be, so to speak, 'literally' or 'pragmatically' interpreted as illustrated by

(S9) All visitors must buy a parking ticket.

Such a statement can naturally be interpreted in a sense which would be explicated by:

(S9*) All visitors who enter by car must buy a parking ticket.

---

[46] Given that one accepts that true assertions can be made by truth denials commenting on items that do not possess any propositional content one should rather say: 'against the background of contents which those items possess or the fact that they do not possess any propositional content'.

According to a, presumably less natural, but not impossible interpretation the universal quantification possesses a strict import so that the sentence should be rather explicated by the paraphrase:

(S9**) All visitors, no matter how they enter, must buy a parking ticket.

A comment on (S9) can pertain alternatively to the content expressed by (S9*) or to the one expressed by (S9**) without presupposing a linguistic ambiguity in the strict sense of this term. Examples like these do not only reveal how easy it is to irritate other people by wilfully imputing imports which were not intended, perhaps not even conceived before as possibilities. They also disclose that sometimes little is achieved by considering exclusively languages or varieties of language that are freed from linguistic ambiguities.

Apart from this, T-comments can even pertain to radically different types of content as evidenced by

(S10) I have worked forty-eight hours.

Interpreted in a literal sense (S10) would convey the thought that the speaker has worked for forty-eight hours, presumably more or less without interruption. But by using a sentence like (S10) one can equally convey a 'conversational implicature' that could be paraphrased by

(S10*) I have completed an amount of work which would be normally achieved in (almost) double the time.

A T-comment expressing assent or dissent concerning (an utterance of) (S10) might not, and presumably would not, linguistically reveal whether it pertains to its literal import or to some conversationally induced import.

Considered in this light the following thesis should appear acceptable: if the existence of different types of content is admitted at all a T-comment can, in principle at least, pertain either to a linguistically indicated content or to a holistic content or to different specimens of linguistic or holistic content – without requiring any difference of its (linguistic) meaning. A corollary of this tenet is that the number of theoretical possibilities can increase in correlation with the number of T-comments that function as (direct or indirect) objects of a T-comment.

Reflections on the argument II*) discussed in section II.B) support this contention. Assuming that (the truth ascription of) Ψ pertains to the linguistically indicated content of Ω and (the truth denial of) Ω to the linguistic content[47] of Ψ the situation is similar as the one that had been ascertained above regarding Σ. Both items indirectly dispute the truth of their own linguistic content. Given, however, that Ψ is taken as pertaining to the linguistic content of Ω, the latter item could be also interpreted as pertaining to the holistic content of its counterpart Ψ, claiming that Ψ, by attributing truth to the linguistic content of Ω and denying the truth of its own truth ascription, is bound to fail in any attempt to impart a truth. In this case it would be consistent to attribute the property of expressing a truth to Ω but not to Ψ. As a matter of fact, even Ω could be interpreted in a way that implies an inconsistency of its holistic content: Ω, by denying the truth of the linguistic content expressed by Ψ might entail a denial of its own truth denial. Instead of taking the increase of theoretical possibilities as a symptom of the untenability of the envisaged account, we consider it more appropriate to conclude that T-comments intrinsically exhibit a sort of indeterminacy which could be diminished by resorting to explanatory paraphrases, in particular expressions of the form 'By affirming/negating that p, S expresses* something which is (not) true'.

Considering against this background the example dealt with in I), one can be tempted to object that even with respect to Σ one must concede the possibility that the item pertains to its own holistic content and thereby conveys a truth relying on the fact that it is inconsistent to deny the truth of its own content and simultaneously deny (the truth of) this denial. Even in light of the circumstance that it is rather unusual that one and the same item is used for making concurrently statements of comment pertaining to different levels, there is no need

---

[47] Henceforth the term 'linguistic content' abbreviates 'linguistically indicated content'.

to categorically reject this possibility. If one admits this possibility one is bound to accept that one and the same T-comment possesses a plurality of holistic contents differing in truth value. This is, however, perfectly compatible with the stance that if a difference of truth value can be ascertained a difference of propositional content must be acknowledged too. The tenet, on the other hand, that one and the same linguistic item can exhibit a plurality of contents without presupposing linguistic ambiguity finds independent support with respect to T-comments in particular.

(7)

Against this backdrop, one can equally ascertain how it is feasible to make consistent truth denials with respect to the items appearing in a(n infinite) 'Yablo-sequence'. The decisive point is that if such denials are couched in formulations, such as

> All members of a Yablo-sequence are untrue.
> All elements within a Yablo-series fail to express a truth.

the verbalizations must permit particular (sorts of) explications which cannot be equivalent to

> That which all members of a Yablo-series express is untrue.

but only to

> All members of a Yablo-series by expressing what they express express* something which is not true.

or more specifically:

> All members of a Yablo-series, inasmuch as they express that that which all subsequent members express fails to be true, fail to express* something true.

The last formulation makes fully explicit that, given that all the members in the series negate the truth of the explicitly expressed content of all the subsequent members, they cannot exhibit a true holistic content. The reason is evidently that truth of any member would require on the one hand that all subsequent members fail to express anything true and on the other hand that that which all the members express, namely that all subsequent members fail to express anything true, is untrue. This is inconsistent. Accordingly one can assign truth to a T-comment that gainsays the truth of the holistic content of the elements in a Yablo-series without denying the truth of their explicitly expressed content. Even the possibility exists that some 'meta-comment' exhibiting the described characteristics occurs within a Yablo-sequence. But this supposition would entail that its holistic content differs from that of those members implying truth denials with respect to the linguistic contents of the members subsequent to them. But a T-comment denying the truth of a true T-comment of this sort would entail an additional divergence regarding holistic content: It would amount to a negation of the truth of a T-comment which truly disclaims that an inconsistent holistic content cannot be true and has to be assessed as failing to be true on that account. Again the principle that deviance in truth value presupposes deviance of content is not violated. But the possibility of the existence of phrasings potentially embodying an incalculable amount of divergent contents which in principle can be accounted for by various explicatory paraphrases is an inevitable consequence of the proposed account.

Considering this, one can be prompted to object that at least with respect to T-comments arranged in an infinite Yablo-series the concept of a holistic content amounts to an absurdity. For illustrating the problem it suffices to consider the supposition that all denials of the individual elements exclusively pertain to the linguistic content of the subsequent members. Isn't it obvious that on that condition any member's being true by requiring that all subsequent members fail to be true presupposes that for every member some member exists which does (not not) express a truth? This means with respect to the first member M_1 in particular that, since the explicit content of all subsequent members must be untrue, some member M_m which directly or indirectly follows its subsequent member M_2 exists which expresses a truth; since this in its turn requires that the linguistic contents of all members subsequent to M_m are untrue some member M_{m+n} must occur following the member which immediately follows M_m in the series that expresses a truth, and so on ad infinitum. Doesn't this amount to the supposition that M_1 possesses an infinitely complex holistic content and that the same holds true for any other member of the sequence? — Against this it can be retorted as follows: If the assumption of an infinite series of T-comments does not amount to absurdity, why should we suppose that the assumption of a content of infinite complexity amounts to an absurdity? If, on the other hand, the assumption of contents of infinite complexity is absurd, should not the assumption of an (actually) infinite series of T-comments also fall into discredit?[48] Anyhow, if a deviousness resides in the idea of a content of unlimited complexity there might exist an additional reason for refusing to attribute truth to the elements in a Yablo-sequence or for attributing absence of truth to them.

Leaving aside these questions one might still insist that the mere supposition of the existence of contents of extremely high complexity suffices for discrediting the hypothesis. If a type of content which allegedly plays a pivotal role for truth-value assessments can exhibit a degree of complexity which renders it unidentifiable for normal beings, it threatens to annihilate its supposed function. As a finite but extremely long Yablo-series could thwart all attempts to completely specify its holistic content, it might appear mysterious how any normal being should ever be in a position to definitely ascertain questions of truth or untruth concerning its elements. — It is not difficult to see that and why this criticism is unwarranted: It would suffice to consider only the first member of a series if one only knew that the subsequent members possess exactly the same import even ignoring how long the sequence is. Knowing that the first member disputes the truth of the explicitly expressed content of the subsequent members and knowing that the following member equally disputes the truth of the linguistic content of the members following it, one can definitely establish that the initial member must fail to be a truth, that the same must hold true

48 If that were the case the situation envisaged in the Yablo-paradox would not satisfy the postulates stipulated for the recognition of genuine truth paradoxes.

for the second member if another member possessing the same import follows it and so on. If in any conjunction of propositions one detects only two elements which are mutually incompatible one can ascertain in advance that the complex conjunction must fail to be true irrespective of the identity of the remaining members. Hence full and comprehensive specifications of (holistic) content are not necessarily required for achieving categorical determinations of truth value.

Besides, even impossibility of categorical truth-value determination does not entail absolute ignorance concerning truth condition. This can be easily seen by considering a slight modification of the famous Epimenides paradox: If Epimenides the Cretan had said:

(S11) Nothing which any other Cretan apart from me has said is true.

one is surely not in a position to ascertain whether (S11) expresses a truth or not, as long as one does not know anything about utterances made by other Cretans. But one can definitely establish that *if* any other Cretan had said something true *then* (S11) cannot express any truth. For vindicating conditional truth assessments of that kind, understanding of the mere linguistic meaning can be sufficient even in the absence of knowledge of a holistic content. (This phenomenon deserves to be indicated in passing because it possesses significance for the methodology of empirical investigations of intellectual traditions.) Alternatively, one might say that linguistic understanding is apt to provide "truth-condition templates", schemata like

If there is a p such that some Cretan other than Epimenides says that p and it is true that p, then (S11) expresses an untruth.

If there is no p such that any Cretan other than Epimenides says that p and it is true that p, then (S11) expresses a truth.

Schemata of this kind furnish guiding lines for evaluating possible contents with respect to their potential of verifying, falsifying, confirming or casting doubt on (statements made by) sentences like (S11).

(8)

The distinctive feature of the 'genuine' Epimenides paradox is that its starting point does not refer to specific sentences uttered or statements made by other people. In order to clarify the matter let us consider the situation against the background of the sentence

(S12) No proposition is true,
in other words:
Every proposition is untrue, or
Every proposition is such that it is not true.

Let us take the term 'proposition' in the sense of either 'proposition that is ever expressed' or 'proposition that has been expressed till the present time and including the present time'. The reason is that an assumption to the effect that no proposition is true can amount to an absurdity because it could be argued that for any untrue proposition there must be a negated counterpart which is not untrue or true. In the introductory section I of this essay we stipulated that assumptions of absurdities are not to be permitted as bases for the derivation of truth paradoxes. In contrast the suppositions that no true proposition expressed at some time exists or that among the propositions that have been formulated in the past and at present none exists which is true are probably, and hopefully, empirically wrong but not absurd or inconsistent. On the other hand, no restriction must be imposed on the range of the quantification. This means that (S12) is not equivalent to

No proposition which is not expressed by (S12) is true.

but can be elucidated by

Absolutely no proposition is true.

For facilitating an assessment against the background of ordinary intuitions the following chain of reasoning will be presented without employing uncommon technical symbols and the leftmost numbers signal (as often before) the assumptions on which pertinent lines depend, if there are any such assumptions:

X)

1	(1)	No proposition is true.	A
1	(2)	The proposition that no proposition is true is not true.	1 UE[49]
1	(3)	It is not the case that no proposition is true.	3 Tp/p[50]
1	(4)	No proposition is true & It is not the case that no proposition is true.	1,3 &I
	(5)	It is not true that no proposition is true.	1,4 RAA
	(6)	Ergo: There is some proposition which is true.	

This outcome is apt to trigger the following consideration: As the proposition that no proposition is true cannot be true because it involves an internal inconsistency the result formulated in line (6) can only be interpreted as meaning that some true proposition exists which differs from the proposition that no proposition is true. As indicated above, it is highly probable that, as a matter of fact, some other true proposition has been articulated in the past. Nevertheless, the idea that the proposition that some true proposition has been expressed at the present time or before constitutes an *a priori* truth — after all, line (6) does not depend on any assumption — appears eccentric. Should we assume that it must be *a priori* certain that (S12), or some synonymous item, is not the first sentence that has been articulated in the history of the universe? In addition to this one can demonstrate that a parallel argument could be construed employing a sentence of the form

No proposition expressed in context C is true.

where 'C' represents a description which is so specific that at most one utterance occurs in the pertinent context. Accordingly, one should ask: What goes wrong in the argument presented in X)?

In the light of the principle that every proposition entails itself one can easily ascertain that the assumption of the first line in X) entails

---

49 According to rule of universal quantifier elimination (UE). Note that the first line is to be understood in such a way that the proposition that no proposition is true has been expressed at the latest when the line has been written down.

50 In accordance with the principle that '(The proposition) that p is true' is equivalent to 'p'.

both that no proposition is true and that it is not true that no proposition is true. Thus the truth of this contradiction can be regarded as a necessary requirement for the possibility of the truth of the proposition expressed in (S12). Using the terminology explained earlier it can be contended that the truth of the proposition that no proposition is true means* not only that the proposition that no proposition is true is true but also that the proposition that no proposition is true is not true. This means that the proposition's being true means* both that no proposition is true and that it is not true that no proposition is true. Given that assuming a proposition means* to assume that the proposition is true, one can claim that making the assumption formulated in the first line of X) means* to make the assumption that it is both the case that no proposition is true and the case that it is not true that that no proposition is true, in other words that it is both the case and not the case that no proposition is true. Hence taking into account and making explicit what treating the first line as an assumption means*, one obtains the following representation of the argument:

X*)

1	(1) No proposition is true & It is not the case that no proposition is true.	A
1	(2) It is not the case that no proposition is true.	&E
1	(3) There is some proposition which is true.	

The result obtained in (3) of X*) is not disconcerting because this line depends on the assumption of the first line. It only reflects the tenet that from contradictions propositions can be validly derived irrespective of whether the consequences are true or not.

It is not difficult to discern that a marked difference exists between that what it means* that a proposition is true, what a proposition's being true means* or, maybe, what a proposition means* on the one hand and on the other hand the question what a linguistic item expressing a proposition means. Evidently the expressions

'No proposition is true.'

and

> 'No proposition is true and the proposition (itself) that no proposition is true is not true.'

do not mean the same. Nevertheless, the latter expression can be regarded as articulating what the fact that the range of the quantification in (S12) includes the proposition expressed by (S12) means*. Hence the holistic content of (S12), which amounts to the content of the last sentence quoted above or of the first line in X*), yields an explication of the most important consequence of the pertinent character of the quantification or of its meaning*.

Those results facilitate an assessment of the 'genuine' Epimenides paradox that was presented as argument VI) in section II.D). It possesses the distinguishing feature that references to (TE2) or rules traceable to (TE2) are absent. As the individual derivational steps in VI) appear irreproachable it can be presumed that the problems lie elsewhere.

It is apparently taken for granted that the first assumption:

$$K[\forall x\,(Kx \rightarrow Fx)]$$

to be read as:

> (The proposition) that everything which is asserted by a Cretan is false is asserted by a Cretan.

articulates a possible situation. It has to be taken in this way because otherwise the derivability of an incredible consequence would lose its paradoxical character. Here 'K' ought to be interpreted in the sense of 'is asserted by a Cretan' and not in the sense of 'is said by a Cretan', for it is not unproblematic to treat 'assert' and 'say' as interchangeable in this context.[51] The verb 'say' can be employed in a way according to which 'A Cretan says that everything asserted by Cretans is false'

---

[51] In Künne 2013 the formula '$\forall x\,(Kx \rightarrow Fx)$' is paraphrased on p. 54 by 'Everything that is asserted by a Cretan is false' [Alles, was von einem Kreter *behauptet* wird, ist falsch] and according to p. 55 the first line of VI) should express that a Cretan says that Cretans only assert falsehoods [ein Kreter *sagt*, dass Kreter nur Falsches behaupten]. He clearly wants '*sagt*' to be taken in the sense of '*behauptet*'.

would mean that a Cretan uses linguistic expressions which are synonymous with 'everything asserted by Cretans is false'. Understood in *this* sense, the assumption that a Cretan says that everything asserted by Cretans is false certainly represents a possibility. But does this suffice for guaranteeing the possibility that a Cretans *asserts* that everything asserted by Cretans is false? Can it be taken for granted that by *assertively* uttering certain words nothing else is asserted than that which those words express?

According to line 4 in VI) the assumption that everything asserted by a Cretan is false entails that if a Cretan asserts that everything asserted by a Cretan is false then this, viz that everything asserted by a Cretan is false, is false. Hence the holistic content of sentences like

(S13) Nothing a Cretan asserts is true.
(S14) Everything a Cretan asserts is false.

is not the (linguistically) expressed content of those sentences but is equivalent to a content which entails

> Everything a Cretan asserts is false, and if a Cretan asserts that everything a Cretan asserts is false then it is false that everything a Cretan asserts is false.

or in the notation employed in VI):

$$\forall x\,(Kx \rightarrow Fx)\ \&\ (K[\forall x(Kx \rightarrow Fx)] \rightarrow F[\forall x(Kx \rightarrow Fx)])$$ [52]

This formulation makes explicit the fact that the quantification in items like (S13) or (S14) is unrestricted; it articulates what it means* that the proposition intended to be expressed by those sentences is true. Thus the content of the assertions made in utterances of (S13) or (S14) does not coincide with their linguistically expressed content. If

52 Note that the submitted formulation presents merely an explication of the import of the universal quantification and on this account need not represent the holistic content of the pertinent sentence if it were uttered by a Cretan. As a matter of fact, whereas the formulation could specify the holistic content of sentences uttered by Non-Cretans, the holistic content of the sentence uttered by a Cretan — and the content of the assertion made by a Cretan assertively uttering it — can be more specific. More on this will be said below.

somebody assertively utters one of those sentences he asserts a proposition which is equivalent to the conjunction specified above. This means that in the pertinent situation it is not the case that nothing else is asserted than that which the words express. To be sure, under these circumstances the holistic content of an assertion can differ drastically from anything which someone employing a sentence 'has in mind'. But against those who want to employ this fact for discrediting the account it should be maintained that exclusive orientation by what subjects have in mind when they linguistically express something generally amounts to poor methodology.

It is possible that someone utters the sentence:

(S15) It is extremely cold here now.

without possessing the slightest idea concerning his location or the precise date of his utterance. But this does not refute the tenet that it can be a most important task of interpretation to identify location and date against the background of an external or even objective perspective. At any rate, such identifications are vital for making decisions about the truth or lack of truth of what has been said, or rather, asserted.[53] For assessing the truth value of a T-comment formulated by

(S16) That is true.

it is indispensable to identify the proposition referred to. Among T-comments there is a special variety which could be christened 'blank T-comments'. Somebody might assertively utter the sentence

(S17) Whatever the president answers to the question will be untrue.

and at the same time not know what the president in fact said or will say. The statement is made on the basis of the assumption that one can presume in advance that the president gives an untrue answer. It is at least not counter-intuitive to hypothesize that someone making a blank

---

[53] This need not be always the case if indexical elements are involved: With respect to the sentence

If it is Monday today it will be Tuesday tomorrow.

truth-value assessments can dispense with identifications of reference.

T-comment asserts something that transcends the linguistically expressed content. Accordingly, the proposition that it is not true that the president in question has never met the Russian ambassador would be part of the asserted content if the president were to say:

(S18) I have never met the Russian ambassador.

It is conspicuous that under such circumstances explorations concerning the query of what a speaker or author 'really thought' are irrelevant. For there is nothing in the mind of subjects making blank T-comments which could decide questions of truth. Instead of appealing to linguistic intuitions regarding the word 'assertion' one might rather allow that theoretical considerations play a critical role in the present connection: If one prefers, on theoretical grounds, to connect the concept of assertion and of asserted content most directly with truth and absence of truth then contents of assertions must be items which are not determined by linguistic meaning and mental facts.

Replacing

$$\forall x\,(Kx \rightarrow Fx)$$

in VI) consistently by

$$\forall x\,(Kx \rightarrow Fx)\ \&\ (K[\forall x(Kx \rightarrow Fx)] \rightarrow F[\forall x(Kx \rightarrow Fx)])$$

yields again the result that the content of the Cretan's remark leads to an inconsistency and cannot be true — given that inconsistencies can never be true. On the other hand it can be ascertained that instead of the disconcerting consequence that (at least) some truth must have been asserted by some Cretan one now merely needs to admit a (fairly plausible) principle to the effect that if something is a truth then it cannot (simultaneously) be a falsehood if asserted by a Cretan.[54] The counterpart of the final line 11 in VI) which previously read:

$$K[\forall x\,(Kx \rightarrow Fx)] \rightarrow F[\forall x\,(Kx \rightarrow Fx)]$$

---

54 Note that this does not imply a denial of the possibility that the very act of an assertion can make the asserted content false. Consider an assertive utterance of 'At this very moment nobody asserts anything'.

> If it is asserted by a Cretan that everything asserted by a Cretan is false, then it is false that everything asserted by a Cretan is false.

must now read:

$$K[\forall x\,(Kx \rightarrow Fx)\ \&\ (K[\forall x\,(Kx \rightarrow Fx)] \rightarrow F[\forall x\,(Kx \rightarrow Fx)])]$$
$$\rightarrow$$
$$F[\forall x\,(Kx \rightarrow Fx)\ \&\ (K[\forall x\,(Kx \rightarrow Fx)] \rightarrow F[\forall x\,(Kx \rightarrow Fx)])]$$

If we dispense with abbreviations and the notation of formal logic this turns into a compound sentence which is not a jewel of English prose:

> ***If*** it is asserted by a Cretan that
> (both) (i) everything asserted by a Cretan is false and (ii) if it asserted by a Cretan that everything asserted by a Cretan is false then that (namely that everything asserted by a Cretan is false) is false
>
> ***then*** it is false that
> (both) (i) everything asserted by a Cretan is false and (ii) if it asserted by a Cretan that everything asserted by a Cretan is false then that (namely that everything asserted by a Cretan is false) is false.

Notwithstanding the deterring complexity, which merely results from the circumstance that all details are explicitly spelt out, one can clearly assess what the result amounts to. The formal structure reveals that, if a Cretan would assert that which he supposedly asserts, the content of his assertion would be false. But the proposition which is declared to false markedly differs from the previous conclusion. Declared to be false is a proposition to the effect that two things concurrently hold good, namely (i) that everything asserted by a Cretan is false, and (ii) that if a Cretan asserts that everything asserted by a Cretan is false it a falsehood that everything asserted by a Cretan is false. It is easy to recognize that the consequence does not any more possess the paradoxical corollary discerned before. As it is the conjunction of (i) and (ii) and not (i) alone which needs to be false or untrue, it cannot be deduced that something asserted by a Cretan is true. What really follows is something which intuitively appears completely plausible, namely the proposition that if everything asserted by a Cretan is in fact false then this (viz. that everything asserted by a Cretan is false) is a truth (even) if a Cretan asserted (among other things) that everything asserted by a Cretan is false.

This outcome is completely compatible with the assumption that somebody can truly assert that everything asserted by a Cretan is false and that a falsehood is asserted if a Cretan asserts that everything asserted by a Cretan is false. After all, line 11 in VI) merely affirms that this cannot be truly asserted if a Cretan makes an assertion to that effect. This discrepancy can be ascribed to a disparity of holistic content generated in the two different sorts of situations. If a sentence of the form:

If (person) A ϕs that p, then q.

— where 'ϕ' is replaceable by verbs like 'say', 'assert', 'deny' etc. — expresses a truth and is (assertively) uttered by someone, then its holistic content usually amounts to the true conditional proposition (linguistically) expressed by that sentence. As long as, and only as long as the utterer is not A himself, his being related in a way designated by 'ϕs' to the proposition designated by 'that p' does not entail (the truth) of the proposition designated by 'q'. Even if 'q' were replaced by 'not p' a true assertion can be made by the conditional sentence. By assertively uttering a sentence synonymous with

For any p: if A asserts that p then q / not p.

everybody who is not A can assert precisely that which the conditional sentence expresses. If, however, the same sentence were assertively uttered by A, the universal quantification creates the effect that the truth of the consequent proposition constitutes a requirement for the truth of the assertion. Given that the content of the assertion is its holistic content, the asserted content exhibits the form

$((A\ \phi s \text{ that } p) \rightarrow q)\ \&\ q$

whenever A uses a sentence of the form of the first conjunct in order to make an assertion. Hence holistic contents and contents determined by (linguistic) meanings of items containing indexical elements together with circumstances of employment share the property of dependence on context.

These results make it possible to build a bridge between truth paradoxes and *set theoretic paradoxes*. Again it is appropriate to begin with a question of meaning by asking what it means for a set to be a set of all sets which do not contain themselves as elements. A natural answer would be, that some U is a set of sets which do not contain themselves as elements if it can be specified by the following description:

> For all sets x: if x is not an element of x then x is (a set which is) an element of U and if x is an element of U then x is (a set which is) not an element of x.

This formulation fails to reveal which verdict ought to be given about U itself, which is supposed to be a set, but, and this is more important, it does not make explicit, whether the universal quantification should be taken as restricted to sets different from U or whether it does not involve any limitation at all. It is not difficult to find a solution for overcoming this drawback. The following formulation would satisfy the desideratum:

> For all sets x: if x is not an element of x then x is an element of U and if x is an element of U then x is not an element of x, and this holds equally good if x is identical with U.

or more explicitly:

> For all sets x: if x is not an element of x then x is an element of U and if x is an element of U then x is not an element of x, and if x is identical with U, then if x is not an element of x then x is an element of U and if x is an element of U then x is not an element of x.

As propositions of the form: ‘For all x: Fx and Gx’ entail ‘For all x: Gx’, it can be derived that

> For all sets x: if x is identical with U, then if x is not an element of x then x is an element of U and if x is an element of U then x is not an element of x.

By replacing the variable ‘x’, bound by the universal quantifier, by ‘U’ in the open sentence, one obtains:

> if U is identical with U, then if U is not an element of U then U is an element of U and if U is an element of U then U is not an element of U.

This means nothing but:

> if U is identical with U, then U is an element of U if and only if U is not an element of U.

This makes plain that the proposition can be true at best if U is not identical with U, and, given that everything which exists needs to be identical with itself, it follows that the requirement could be met at best if the set U does not exist — if one does not want to adopt the audacious tenet that sets in general are non-existent.

In view of the fact that it is commonly supposed that a set of all sets not containing themselves as elements cannot exist, one might wonder what is achieved by replacing the first less explicit wording by the more explicit variants. In reply to this one can say that the explicit variants enable one to localize the contradiction. It can happen that one first specifies some idea or concept, say the concept of a prime number which is greater than 31 and smaller than 37, and after having performed some investigation concerning the ‘world of natural numbers’ one detects that no item falls under the specified concept. By resorting to the explicit varieties of the specification one makes clear that the situation regarding the concept of a set of all sets not containing themselves is different. The contradiction is, so to speak, inbuilt in the concept itself. It emerges on the basis of a mere reflection about the question as to what the non-restricted nature of the quantification amounts to: It amounts to the postulate that exactly the same principle which regulates decisions of class membership concerning U for sets in general should regulate such decisions also with respect to U. One might say, that the considered paradox is essentially not a problem of sets but a problem of meaning.[55] This in its turn can furnish an explanation — or partial explanation — for the intuition that an affinity exists between truth paradoxes and paradoxes of set theory.[56]

(9)

It is a characteristic feature of the examples considered in section II.E) above that equally consistent alternative truth-value assignments can be made and the choice between them seems completely arbitrary. For an assessment of the situation it suffices to focus on the situation where two persons A and B mutually ascribe lack of truth to linguistic items produced by them.

If the property of not expressing something true is attributed to a linguistic unit that possesses a content, it is not reasonable to interpret it as disputing any content to that item. It must be presumed, at least by default, that the denial implies an ascription of untruth to some content. Regarding the example of two 'colleagues' mutually ascribing untruth to a linguistic item produced by the other, the most

---

55 The problem would not arise in the same manner if it were supposed that the general way of specifying classes or sets should not be given by expressions of the form: 'The (set of) x, such that Fx', but rather by 'The (set of) x, such that Fx & for all y: if y = x, then x does not contain y as member' or: 'The (set of) x, such that Fx & for all y: if y is member of x, then x is not member of y'. That would be legitimate, if the relation of set membership should be irreflexive or asymmetric; in this case the expanded formulations would merely make those facts explicit set membership should be irreflexive or asymmetric; in this case the expanded formulations would merely make those facts explicit.

56 The explicit description amounting to:

U is a set of all sets which do not contain themselves as elements and which contains itself as element if and only if it does not contain itself as element

makes merely manifest that the less explicit specification:

U is a set of all sets which do not contain themselves as elements

(latently) exhibits a similar inconsistency as, for example:

U is a set containing only sets and containing words as elements.

natural assumption is that each remark is about the explicitly expressed content of the sentence token produced by the other speaker. Hence A, by expressing that no item expressing a truth is produced by B, can be taken as asserting that the content of B's remark to the effect that no item expressing a truth is produced by A, is an untruth. This in its turn implies that A's remark to the effect that no item expressing a truth is produced by B is a true remark, that the proposition he himself expresses is true. The same can be said *mutatis mutandis* about B and the linguistic item produced by him. Each of A and B, by ascribing lack of truth to the content of the remark of his colleague, claims truth regarding his own remark. It emerges as a result that the holistic contents are not exhausted by the implied denials. Rather, the sentence uttered by A possesses a holistic content to the effect that no item expressing a truth is produced by B *and* that he himself expresses a truth by saying that no item expressing a truth is produced by B. The sentence uttered by B possesses as its holistic content the conjunctive proposition that no item expressing a truth is produced by A *and* that he himself expresses a truth by saying that no item expressing a truth is produced by A. Assertive utterances always involve a claim of truth with respect to something expressed by them, but, or course, normally the proposition that one is expressing a truth is not an ingredient of the content of one's utterances. By assertively uttering the sentence

Napoleon Bonaparte made war on Prussia.

one asserts that Napoleon Bonaparte made war on Prussia but not that one asserts a truth by assertively uttering the sentence 'Napoleon Bonaparte made war on Prussia'. The content, be it linguistic or holistic, does not contain metalinguistic ingredients under these circumstances. But the situation differs in the case of the T-comments under consideration. Here one is entitled to contend that all pertinent items, i.e. both the sentence uttered by A and the sentence uttered by B, fail to express a truth. The crucial reason lies in the second component of the holistic contents according to which each of the two adversaries ascribes truth to his own remark. The reason for refraining from assigning truth to those ingredients is that no independent objective support exists for such an assignment: Any conceivable ground for attributing truth to the linguistically expressed content which ascribes lack of truth to its counterpart relies on an attribution of truth to itself and generates a vicious circle. Hence the situation closely resembles situations in which a sentence attributes truth to itself or two sentences mutually ascribe truth to each other (and to nothing else)[57]: There is no truth ground which does not entail the truth of the item to be evaluated.[58] (The idea of a set S which is such that it only contains itself as an element embodies a similar problem. If the set S contains only the set S as an element then the set which it contains as its element must contain the set S as its element and so on. How should it be possible to ascertain the identity of this set, given that the identity of sets depends on (the identity) of the elements they contain?)

An explanation of the possibility of correctly attributing absence of truth to both members of the pair was given before: A sentence expressing a denial of truth regarding the sentences produced by A and B as well as the statements made by them can be used in a way that it pertains to the holistic imports of those items. If a third person C expresses a denial of this kind he does not dispute the truth of the linguistically expressed content of the sentences uttered by A and B

[57] A linguistic unit can be true or express a truth only by being related to some content that is capable of being a truth. But a content to the effect that some linguistic item is true or expresses a truth is not by itself a content which can represent a truth. The fact that truths can be asserted by using expressions which merely express attributions or denials of truth regarding linguistic items does not yield a valid counterargument. Even by employing 'yes' or 'no' one can under appropriate circumstances assert something.

[58] The proposition

(i) that it is true that Napoleon made war on Prussia

does not entail the proposition

(ii) that the (English) sentence 'Napoleon made war on Prussia' is true.

For one thing, (i) could hold good even if no (English) sentence expressing this fact — or any fact — had ever been produced. More importantly, a derivation of (ii) from (i) would require (TE2) as an additional premise. (i) can be considered as an independent ground for the linguistic item's being true or expressing a truth.

but the truth of their holistic contents. C thereby disclaims truth to the disjunctive proposition that A expresses a truth and B an untruth or B expresses a truth and A an untruth. By denying such disparities C's denial is associated with a holistic content differing from the contents associated with the original remarks made by A and by B respectively. One might contend that no compelling reason exists for interpreting the sentences uttered by the two adversaries in the manner envisaged above. However, if one assumes that, for example, B's remark differs from the one made by A by the fact that it disputes the holistic content of its counterpart and that accordingly B expresses a truth whereas A does not, then the principle that differences of truth value entail differences of (some) content remains unaffected. If both remarks were directed against holistic contents in the same way, one avoids admission of any unfounded bias by dismissing truth regarding both. As a matter of fact, when confronted with truth denials one might not be in a position to definitely ascertain their holistic content. There might be nothing which could justify any categorical decision between different alternatives; so that one can at best attribute truth or untruth under various explicatory interpretations. If based on those considerations a denial of (categorical) truth is expressed, it possesses yet another holistic content.

V. Outlook

The account of truth paradoxes offered in this essay is conservative inasmuch as it does not question the validity of any elementary classical rule of derivation. The fact that our account does not involve a rejection of 'Classical Logic' does not imply any claim to the effect that Classical Logic gives a correct account of deductive reasoning in general. It does not imply either that non-conservative accounts of truth paradoxes are not worth pursuing. But the first segment of argument V) in section II above, which has the proposition that Napoleon Bonaparte was an orthodox Hindu in its final line, reveals that, as long as the general validity of two principles connecting meaning with truth is acknowledged, paradoxical outcomes emerge even if the classical rule of *reductio ad absurdum* is not appealed to. This makes it very natural to question the validity of these 'non-logical' principles.

On the other hand, the propagated stance of questioning (TE1) or (TE2) or both, together with [P1] and [P2], is quite moderate. So far, (TE1) and [P1] have not been contested. The censure was exclusively directed against (TE2) and [P2]. Even this criticism was modest because it discards (TE2) merely in the form in which it was originally envisaged. The distinction between linguistically expressed content and holistic content allows us to specify a relation between linguistic items and holistic content, which could be designated by the term 'express*'. Then it turns out that both (TE1) and (TE2) could still be maintained with respect to the examples of truth paradox we considered if the term 'express' were consistently replaced by 'express*'. (Admittedly, in actual practice it is often not required to signal the difference explicitly.)

At this point one might suspect that the revision is too restrained. Doesn't it obscure problems that arise even with (TE1) and [P1]? Here is an object of comparison. Allegedly, the French king Louis XIV uttered the sentence:

(19F) L'état, c'est moi.

Given that (19F) is synonymous with

(19E) I am the state.

one is entitled to assert that both the type sentence (19F) and the token of (19F) uttered by Louis XIV mean what (19E) means in English. But are we entitled to *derive* from this the following conclusion?

(*) If (19F) (as uttered by Louis XIV) expresses that I am the state and (19F) (as uttered by Louis XIV) thereby expresses a truth, then I am the state.

or:

(**) If Louis XIV said that I am the state and Louis XIV thereby said something true, then I am the state.

To be sure, a speaker assertively uttering one of these sentences can be credited with saying something true. But it is clearly inappropriate to affirm that the truth of (*) or (**) can be derived from the supposition that Louis XIV uttered a sentence which means (in French) the same as 'I am the state' (in English). By assertively uttering (19F) the French monarch did definitely not *intend* to say something which entails that any vintner in the Provence would express a truth if he were to utter a sentence which means exactly the same as (19F), nor did the king say anything a vintner might say by using a sentence possessing the same meaning as the sentence used by the monarch. What can be legitimately derived is only that Louis XIV by employing (19F) created a situation which can be correctly described by

(†) Louis XIV said / uttered a sentence which expresses that he himself, Louis XIV, is the state.

It should be obvious that the import of the expressions 'say' in [P1] and 'express' in (TE1) can only be equivalent to the import of those terms in (†), – an import which does not license the substitution of (19E) in the that-clauses, even though (19E) has the same linguistic meaning as (19f). Now this observation confirms our denial of the claim that the possibility that a Cretan employs words *meaning the same as* 'no Cretan ever asserts anything true' implies the possibility that any Cretan *asserts* that no Cretan ever asserts anything true.

Nevertheless, there remains a difference between (TE1) and (TE2). The latter is acceptable as a general principle at best if a relationship connecting linguistic items with holistic imports is hypothesized. The former is valid even in the version where 'express' is not substituted by 'express*'. The same holds good, *mutatis mutandis*, for [P2] and [P1].

It might be contended that our account of the truth paradoxes fails because it postulates contents as bearers of absolute, not relativized, truth values that do not comply with the intuitive principle of linguistic compositionality which can (informally) be conveyed by the slogan

> The meaning of a complex expression is determined by the meanings of its (immediate) constituents and the mode of their composition.

But even if the principle of compositionality as conveyed by the slogan holds for *linguistic* meanings (which is by no means obvious), our account of the truth paradoxes implies at most that there is *some* kind of content that does not comply with compositionality as conveyed by the slogan, and this is something that should be accepted on all sides. The so-called *conversational implicatures* of an utterance are not strictly determined by the conventional linguistic meaning of the sentence used in the utterance. This observation does not by itself militate against the thesis that the items conveying conversational implicatures also possess a 'literal sense' which *is* compositionally determined. According to our account, the same holds *mutatis mutandis* for *holistic meanings* and T-comments whose truth evaluation requires appeal to such meanings.

The account of the truth paradoxes recommended in this essay may seem to require rejection of the biconditional truth schema

> s is true in L if and only if p

where the place-holder 's' is to be substituted by a (revealing) designator of a declarative sentence in L (e.g. its quotation name) and the place-holder 'p' is to be replaced by a *translation* of that sentence into the metalanguage (English, in our case) that is employed in the biconditional.[59] Now the felicitousness of employing 'is true' as a predicate of sentences is questionable, and it was implicitly questioned above. But it is more important to note that it is far from obvious that our account entails a rejection of the biconditional truth schema. First of all, it requires at most a restriction to those truth candidates that are not self-referential T-comments. Second, it is not even clear that it demands such a stricture. If one applies the biconditional truth schema one invokes the notion of translation, and one can argue that the schema can be applied even to self-referential T-comments if one invokes an appropriate concept of translation. Using the terminology employed in this essay one can say that in the realm of T-comments adequateness of translation does not require identity of sense (linguistic meaning or linguistic meaning plus contextual parameters) but rather identity of holistic meaning. In this way the more comprehensive issue of the nature of translation comes into play, and one comes to recognize that the topic of the paradoxes induced by T-comments turns out to be part of a topic that is relevant for the humanities in general.

Not only in ordinary contexts but even in scientific contexts T-comments exhibiting some sort of self-reference play at best a marginal role. This might be taken to show that the distinction between one kind of meaning that pertains to linguistic items and another kind of meaning that pertains to entities which can be designated by expressions of the form 'A's being F' and 'that A is F' possesses at best quite limited relevance. A preliminary move to dispel this

---

[59] As is well known, this schema is part and parcel of 'Convention T' (formulated by Tarski), according to which a formally correct definition of 'true' for a given object language L in some metalanguage (e.g. English) is materially adequate if and only if it implies all sentences which can be obtained from the schema by appropriate substitutions. — Cf., among others, Sainsbury 1988:139 or Künne 2003:183.

suspicion consists in pointing out that at least the general distinction between meaning pertaining to linguistic items and meaning pertaining to non-linguistic items can certainly not be dismissed as negligible. After all, the realm of meaning pertaining to non-linguistic items is not exhausted by meaning pertaining to entities denoted by terms of the two forms mentioned above. It encompasses material objects, processes and events such as an accumulation of clouds that means rain, actions and kinds of behaviour like remaining silent in reaction to a question, and states of affairs like the fact that smoke is to be seen on the hill. Furthermore, substitution instances of 'A's being F' or 'that A is F', where 'F' is replaced by 'true' show that issues pertaining to non-linguistic items of this particular kind are far from being marginal: if one were to dismiss such issues wholesale as irrelevant one would declare questions of truth to be irrelevant.

According to our analyses of various truth paradoxes, posing questions as to what it means* that some item s expresses a truth is apt to reveal highly important and significant facts about them. They are important because they concern conditions under which a content related to linguistic objects can be assessed as true or untrue. They are significant because they are not always revealed by the linguistic meaning of expressions. The fact that for items, such as Λ, Σ or Ψ above, their expressing a truth means* — or would mean* — that certain contradictions are true cannot be discerned by merely inspecting their linguistic meanings. Reflecting on the explicitly communicated contents of Γ or Δ or grasping the linguistically imparted significance of the individual assumptions formulated in lines (1)–(6) in argument V) in section II.D above does not enable us to recognize that for Γ as well for Δ in those contexts being true means* that particular historical states of affairs obtain which may never have obtained at all. The importance and the significance of explications which answer questions as to what something's being true means* is not restricted to cases where such explications are indispensable for elucidating contents which can be evaluated in the dimension of truth and untruth without leading to inconsistency. In the realm of *historically oriented studies* — a realm that we shall enter in the next essay — the relevance of posing such questions is to a large extent due to the widely distributed phenomena of equivocation and vagueness we encounter in documents of the past. If we wonder whether a formulation we find in such documents represents a (possible) truth or which condition could bestow truth on its content, an explication may be required which just as much transcends the realm of information discernible by ordinary methods of linguistic and philological analysis as do explications revealing truth conditions of linguistic items generating paradoxes of truth. This fact alone makes it imperative to take a firm stand against those who contend that explications which transcend both linguistically conveyed imports and actual intentions of language users are to be eliminated from assessments of traditional doctrines, teachings, theories, or tenets. After all, it is incontestable that in assessments of truth regarding controversial doctrines etc. upheld by our *contemporaries* high importance often accrues to questions as to what they mean*, irrespective of what the words and sentences by which they are expounded mean or what their proponents 'have in mind'. When doctrines etc. advocated in the *past* are at stake the situation does certainly not differ to such an extent that it would be reasonable to neglect questions of truth and of meaning* entirely.

Admittedly, assertions apparently claiming their own falsity, predicates allegedly satisfied by predicates which do not satisfy themselves or terms seemingly referring to sets which contain as elements all sets that do not contain themselves as elements are fairly 'exotic'. But the considerations they call for, considerations about what it means for such items to be true or satisfied or referential, are not only relevant to such outlandish examples. Awareness of the difference between the task of ascertaining linguistic matters of meaning and the task of ascertaining truth and meaning* is also of vital importance when teachings propagated in the course of history are at stake, and the latter task should not be neglected in this field either. Or so I shall argue in the second essay contained in this book.

Appendix

The so-called natural deduction techniques used in this essay stem in essentials from Gentzen, and the style of presentation follows Lemmon 1965. The lines of a derivation are numbered consecutively, '(1)', '(2)' etc. To the *left* of each line the numerals refer to the assumptions (if any) on which the formula in that line depends. Assumptions are premises not depending on any other premise in the derivation. To the *right* of each line acronyms designate the rule justifying the appearance of the formula at that stage and numerals designate the line(s) containing the premise(s) to which the rule is applied.

The following rules of derivation are pertinent in our inquiry:

1. (Rule of) Assumption (A). It allows the introduction of any proposition at any stage of a proof. We write to the left the number of the line itself in which the assumption is made, for it depends on nothing but itself.

2. (Rule of) '&'-Introduction (&I). It allows the derivation of the conjunction 'p & q' if both conjuncts 'p' and 'q' are given as premises. The conclusion depends on the assumption on which the premises 'p' and 'q' depend.

3. (Rule of) '&'-Elimination (&E). It licences the derivation of 'p' as well as of 'q' from their conjunction 'p & q'. Each of these conclusions rest on the same assumptions as the premise.

4. (Rule of) *modus ponendo ponens* (MPP). It allows the derivation of 'q' from the premises 'p → q' and 'p. The conclusion depends on the assumptions on which 'p' and 'p → q' depend.

5. (Rule of) *modus tollendo tollens* (MTT). It licenses the derivation of '¬p' from the premises 'p → q' and '¬q'. The conclusion depends on the assumptions on which 'p → q' and '¬q' depend.

6. (Rule of) Conditional Proof (CP). If ‘p’ is the assumption, or one of the assumptions, on which the derivation of ‘q’ depends, one is entitled to derive in the next step the conditional proposition ‘p → q’. This conclusion no longer depends on ‘p’ but only on the other assumptions (if any) on which the derivation of ‘q’ was based.

7. (Rule of) *reductio ad absurdum* (RAA). If from the assumption ‘p’ or from several assumptions ‘p_1’, ‘p_2’, ..., ‘p_n’ a contradiction, that is, a formula of the form ‘q & ¬q’ can be derived, then we may derive the negation of ‘p’, that is, ‘¬p’, or the negation of one of the several assumptions, e.g. ‘¬p_2’. The conclusion no longer depends on the assumption it negates but only on the other assumptions (if any) on which the derivation of ‘q & ¬q’ was based. Presupposing, reasonably enough, that a (genuine) contradiction cannot be true and that the rules appealed to in its derivation are deductively correct, the assumption, or one of the assumptions, on which its derivation depends has got to be false. If the derivation depends on several assumptions, RAA does not tell us which assumption should be negated.

8. (Rule of) Universal Quantifier-Elimination (UE). This is the only rule involving quantifiers that was appealed to in the preceding investigations. It licences substitutions of terms designating individual objects for variables bound by universal quantifiers. The singular conclusion rests on the same assumptions as the universal premise. If something is true of all objects (in a domain) it must equally be true of every individual object (in that domain).

9. (Rule of) Theorem Introduction (TI). This rule permits us to introduce, at any stage of a derivation, a theorem already proved or a substitution instance of such a theorem. In relying on a theorem an argument does not rely on an additional assumption, for a theorem rests on no assumption. — TI is not a basic rule of derivation: it merely enables us to shorten lengthy derivations that only appeal to rules like the eight preceding rules. (TI was implicitly invoked in lines (7) and (8) in argument V) in section II.D)

References

Bocheński, I.M. / Menne, A. 1973. *Grundriß der Logistik.* (UTB 59) Paderborn: Verlag Schöningh.

Clark, M. 2012. *Paradoxes from A to Z.* Third Edition. London and New York: Routledge. German edition: 2012. *Paradoxien von A bis Z.* Stuttgart: Reclam.

Cook, Roy T. 2009. Diagonalization, the Liar Paradox, and the Inconsistency of the Formal System Presented in the Appendix to Frege's Grundgesetze: Volume II. In: Alexander Hieke, Hannes Leitgeb (eds.), *Reduction, Abstraction Analysis,* Proceedings of the International Ludwig Wittgenstein Symposium in Kirchberg 2008. Heusenstamm: Ontos Verlag, pp. 273–288.

Künne, W. 2003. *Conceptions of Truth.* Oxford: Clarendon Press.

—— 2013. *Epimenides und andere Lügner.* Frankfurt am Main: Klostermann Rote Reihe.

Lemmon, E.J. 1965. *Beginning Logic.* London: Nelson.

Oetke C. 2012. *Ascription of Linguistic Properties and Varieties of Content. Two Studies on Problems of Self-Reference.* Stockholm Oriental Studies. 20. Stockholm: Acta Universitatis Stockholmiensis.

—— 2013. Inconsistency, Paradox and Linguistic Content. Did Bhartṛhari offer a Solution for Truth-Paradoxes? In: *Revista de Filosofía de la Universidad de Costa Rica* 52/134: 9–39.

Quine, W.V. 1966 (1976). *The Ways of Paradox and Other Essays.* Cambridge, Massachusetts and London, England: Harvard University Press.

Sainsbury, R.M. 1988. *Paradoxes.* Cambridge: Cambridge University Press.

Sorensen, Roy, A. 1998. 'Yablo's Paradox and Kindred Infinite Liars'. In: *Mind* 107: 137–155.

Yablo, S. 1993. Paradox without self-reference. In: *Analysis* 53: 251–252.

Part Two

Fact, Fake, and Fiction in Historical Interpretation

Prologue

I

The overarching objective of the present essay does not merely consist in substantiating the contention that the scope of potential goals of explorations of intellectual traditions, such as Greek or Indian philosophy, essentially transcends the aim of identifying individual views and accounting for historical changes and developments of ideas and beliefs. An equally important purpose resides in demonstrating that certain prevailing traditions of research concentrating on historical investigations are not only exposed to the risk of unwarranted imbalance, but are even disposed to fall victim to a neglect of significant differences and even confusions in pertinent regards. In so far as the position is advocated that investigations concerning historical traditions must not be narrowed down to the detection of thoughts entertained at certain times it implies the thesis that studies of traditions of thought are not restricted to the ascertainment of facts *if* this term is taken as pertaining to historical incidences or to relations between them. Given that such a restricted understanding of the term tallies with popular conceptions it would be apposite to characterize the fundamental goal of investigations concerning theoretical traditions of the past as consisting in the ascertainment of truths, in a sense of this term which permits to speak of truths of mathematic or (formal) logic.

It is easy to show that there are truths pertaining to theoretical constructs of the past involving reference to items which could be characterized as fictions in the specific sense that they are not or need not be objects whose existence has ever been envisaged in some previous tradition of thought. For example, it is in principle possible to ascertain about some given system of grammatical rules that it permits — or does not permit — the derivation of correct or incorrect linguistic forms, and, given that the system in question is sufficiently specific and explicit, the ascertainability of the pertinent truths does not depend on the question of whether or not the pertinent linguistic items have ever been considered by the creator of the system or by those who accepted it in the past. To be sure, if the theory in question lacks the required degree of explicitness, a definite verdict might be impossible. But even in such cases a lack of determinateness can be established as an objective truth, provided that certain matters of interpretation or exegesis have been definitely settled. It emerges that an awareness of the difference between issues of exegesis on the one hand and other tasks pertaining to truths which are not historical facts on the other hand matters even for specialists who are engaged in studies on intellectual history. Thus the consideration of 'fictitious objects' does not, for that reason alone, amount to a contemplation concerning fakes. As those scholars who — intentionally or unintentionally — suggest the contrary are guilty of promoting developments which can lead to the inferiority of an academic discipline, it is imperative to clearly expose their fault.

It would be a mistake to derive from the preceding exposition that the relevance of a strict separation between tasks of interpretation and tasks of assessing theoretical truths is confined to 'formal systems', such as certain varieties of grammatical theory. Also with respect to studies on systems and theorems of philosophies not couched in formal terms the difference is important. It might happen, though, that for a clear and definite ascertainment of theoretical truths it is unavoidable — or advisable — to (at least partly) reformulate expressions of natural language by resorting to devices of formal languages. In such cases it can occur that even after a most perspicuous consideration of matters of (philological) exegesis different options of formal explication persist among which one cannot single out one particular alternative as the only legitimate one. Nevertheless, as long as the nature of situations of that kind is truthfully assessed, one must not discard the pertinent enterprise as illegitimate. On the other hand, however, a practice, sometimes suggested in studies, is definitely objectionable which consists in depicting some conceivable alternative as corresponding to (real) intentions of some historical figures portraying the remaining options as 'idle possibilities'. It is precisely this habit which implies a fatal transgression from the realm of 'fiction' to the realm of fakes and needs to be contested on that account.

Analyses of positions in games of chess need not be restricted to a registration of moves or game-stages which actually occurred subsequently in a pertinent game or in the preceding history of playing the game. It can, and presumably will, (equally) take into consideration alternative possible moves and game-stages and conceivably evaluate actual moves and positions in the light of such alternative possibilities. Obviously the circumstance that unrealized possibilities come into consideration does not render the undertaking of analysis arbitrary or capricious. For the rules of the game restrict and determine (the sets of) possible subsequent moves and game-stages. Accordingly, one can distinguish between two in principle legitimate categories of assessment which could be indicated by the terms 'historical' and 'analytical (type of account)'. Whereas the former (mainly) confines itself to registering (subsequent) courses of games that actually occurred and perhaps evaluating (preceding) moves and courses of game against their background, accounts of the latter type are characterized by a readiness to take into consideration unrealized, but possible moves and courses of events whenever this is indicated. The distinction can be generalized beyond the realm of analyses of games. Bringing up this matter is not inapposite. One is entitled to affirm that till the present day the mainstream of scholars dealing with Indian traditions of the past have not clearly grasped this elementary type-difference. Consequently it should not come as a surprise if serious, and maybe comparative, investigations concerning the relevance of those two varieties of assessment can hardly be found. The thesis, however, that need for such inquiries exists deserves to find approval.

II

One can distinguish between three approaches of investigating theoretical traditions and their sources. They differ in accordance with the particular way of understanding subject matters which are concerned, such as linguistic theory, issues of metaphysics, ontology, semantics etc.

A) An approach which aspires to re-enact as faithfully as possible the understanding of the subject matter which some writer of a textual source or a particular tradition of reception had attained during some period in the past.

B) An approach which aims at understanding and analysing a theoretical subject matter that has been investigated in the past against the background of theories which are current at the time and in the (cultural) milieu of the person who studies the tradition.

C) An approach which pursues the goal of achieving maximal depth of insight and thoroughness of knowledge about a topic which had been dealt with in traditions of the past by exploiting any sources potentially relevant for this purpose without attaching critical importance to matters of provenance. According to this stance it would be in principle legitimate to exploit thoughts, teachings or theories concerning e.g. literature from any part of the world, including even a researcher's own considerations not derived from elsewhere, and, *mutatis mutandis*, the same holds good if views and theories developed in some, possibly non-Western, tradition pertaining to other areas than literature constitute objects of study.

An unprejudiced view intimates that all three portrayed approaches are warranted in principle, albeit particular contexts or overarching objectives can justify specific choices among the alternatives. If someone pursues the aim of portraying extensive historical connections an adoption of A) can appear preferable because in this manner the danger of failure due to overloading of tasks is reduced. On the other hand, interest in cultural self-criticism can prompt the attribution of relevance to comparative research. Against this background one could, for example, pursue the aim to ascertain whether theories developed in the framework of generative linguistics or rather grammars of the Paninian tradition could present a more elegant or comprehensive account of a range of syntactic phenomena; or whether philosophies created in the tradition of Kant or the later Wittgenstein permit a more insightful assessment of problems debated in India during the first millennium A.D. concerning the existence of a self, etc. It should be evident that investigations of type A) cannot fulfil purposes of this sort by themselves, but an approach of type B) or even a combination of the two approaches could be appropriate.[60] It might seem that approaches of the last type, viz. C), possess significance

60 Approaches of the category B) do not need to satisfy the strict requirement that an understanding must be achieved which exactly reflects the understanding of an original author; it should only be free of relevant misunderstandings. On the other hand, even interpretations which are not completely faithful, particularly readings which render a position stronger than it actually was, can perform a most useful function in contexts of cultural self-criticism, if they reveal that contemporary theories cannot deal with pertinent issues in an optimal manner.

only under a purely theoretical perspective. To be sure, if someone desires to investigate the problem of semantic compositionality and, among other things, wants to ascertain which kinds of meaning or content might comply with a compositionality-principle and which types do not, or if somebody wishes to attain as many insights about the nature of truth paradoxes as possible, he will be well-advised to embark on investigations of this category. But presumably it is a mistake to suppose that studies of type C) are bound to be irrelevant under historical aspects. By achieving optimal competence in some particular subject-matter one is optimally qualified for recognizing facts of absence or of deficiency with respect to traditions of the past; one is enabled to ascertain decisively more than what actually happened in the course of history by realizing that aspects of some subject matter had been ignored or neglected whose discovery would have entailed significant improvements and which presumably possess relevance even under the perspective of the concerned specimens of tradition themselves. The detection of 'missed opportunities' can acquire potential significance on account of the discovery of specific novel problems and questions, such as the question of the factors responsible for pertinent omissions.

A proper implementation of the C-type approach can require the identification of theoretical connections which, in the field of philosophy, might even link different areas, such as ontology, metaphysics and semantics. For example, as long as we have not previously clarified the issue of whether predicates stand to (specific types of) objects in the same way as proper names stand to their bearers, we are not in a position to ascertain whether a tradition advocating an ontology on the basis of presupposing an affirmative answer to this question without considering matters of semantics thereby omitted inquiries concerning an aspect of a problem which is relevant on the tradition's own premises. If one has not examined whether an identification of possible bearers of absolute (not relativized) truth possesses potential relevance for dealing with the problem of truth paradoxes, one is not entitled to contend that traditions touching on issues of truth paradox failed to address questions which were pertinent to themselves. Viewed against this background it emerges that investigations of the last type can be confronted with special and exacting requirements. It follows that for similar reasons as in the case of studies of type A) investigations of category C) are preferably exempted from some of the liabilities which are binding for inquiries of the former sort to avoid failure because of overload of tasks. This desideratum can be implemented, e.g., by assigning to undertakings of the concerned type an obligation to focus in the first place on intensive explorations concerning shorter textual segments, substituting the ideal of historical breadth by the ideal of analytical depth. It is not unreasonable to expect that by practicing 'division of work' the different approaches might fruitfully complement each other in the longer run.

It seems, however, that this view of the matter is not commonly shared — or perhaps it would be more correct to say that certain people are reluctant to see the matter in this way. Phenomena exist which intimate the opinion that, at least if foreign traditions of thought are concerned, approaches of the types B) and C) are improper, not because of irrelevance but on account of general methodological principles. Usually this stance is propagated in rather ambiguous and vague terms, relying often on slogans, such as:

> One must interpret traditions in their own terms.
> Let traditions speak for themselves!
> One has to understand textual sources in their own historical context.

etc. The crucial point is that dictums apparently endorsing approaches of type A) can be interpreted in a number of different ways and that some but by no means all readings amount to wayward demands. There is one particular explication which deserves serious consideration: It implicates the postulate that textual sources should be interpreted, so to speak, 'from inside towards outside'. This means that primary attention ought to be devoted to the intertextual context, sometimes called 'co-text', preferably in a way which takes properties of sequence, such as order of thoughts or of argumentative steps, into account, attributing distinguished relevance to the most immediate co-text. Considerations relating to other works of the same writer occupy the second major rank in the order of priority. Subsequent to those core elements the pre-existing historical and social environment in which some work originated is to be considered for purposes of controlling the plausibility of the obtained results and assigning orders of preference between alternative readings whenever more than one interpretation is licensed according to the previous criteria. Such a postulate would not be pointless because it can be observed that interpreters sometimes fail to pay due attention to intra-textual connections compensating this omission by alleging historical parallels or by directly relating individual textual passages to putative properties of the historical context. On the other hand, it should be obvious that a methodological procedure of the described sort is most congenial to investigations of type A) as well as to undertakings aiming at the identification of communicative intentions of some original speaker or author. The thesis, however, that one thereby provides an exhaustive methodological account which must be binding for all varieties of textual analysis implies an all too sweeping dismissal of other approaches apart from A). A problematic by-effect of this 'historical' stance is in addition that it puts those in an advantaged position who lack the capacities to go beyond a 'traditional understanding'.

III

In a recently published article[61] a more aggressive version of the postulate of accounting for 'historical context' has been propagated which does not merely suffer from the defect of undue vagueness. As far as one can see, it disallows *any* explication which could render it acceptable. On the one hand, the paper shares the deficiency of lacking an elucidation of the idea of 'historical context', failing to differentiate between pertinent conceptual varieties corresponding to alternative explications and omitting needed clarifications regarding their specific methodological functions. On the other hand, it advocates a position which implies that statements to be found in the 'tradition of reception' ('*Rezeptionsgeschichte*') of teachings, theories or arguments or of textual sources where they are articulated possess the same criterial relevance as the methodological devices highlighted in the previous paragraph. To be sure, the pertinent thesis could be understood as involving a stronger or a weaker claim. In the first case, it would amount to the bold contention that for matters of exegesis opinions of individuals representing a history of reception need to be treated exactly like intra-textual properties. In the second case it would mean that views articulated in the '*Rezeptionsgeschichte*' deserve to be treated as a default-criterion in the sense that, whenever pertinent intra-textual evidence is absent and other sources harking back to an identical author are not available, one must treat a history of reception as equivalent to intra-textual evidence. Since the concerned article does not aspire to higher levels of sophistication in this respect, one cannot make a definite decision between the two alternative interpretations. Anyway, what matters is the fact that on both readings the contention is unacceptable and the reasons will be exposed in the first part of this essay.[62]

---

[61] E. Franco 2016.

[62] One ought to realize that the fact that interpreting teachings in the light of their subsequent tradition of reception inevitably involves the risk of imputing

It might be objected that the alleged lack of plausibility and subtlety exhibited by the above portrayed position should render its criticism unnecessary and inappropriate. Against this demur the following response deserves to be given: One must at all cost — and not only in the field of politics — resist the temptation to be fooled into underestimating something, believing that perceptible implausibility, lack of sophistication or oversimplification prevent acceptance. Furthermore, in view of phenomena occurring in the past one cannot blindly rely on the effectiveness of quality control in academic disciplines.[63] In the present context it deserves to be considered in addition that the recent attempt to underpin exaggerated contentions concerning the relevance of history of reception by a rudimentary account of meaning makes it worthwhile to subject semantic issues to a rigorous inspection.

The second essay dedicated to a detailed survey of a previous debate concerning a specific topic in the area of Indian theoretical

---

distorted pictures concerning the recognition of problems is not exclusively due to the possibility of an increase of *awareness* of problems, i.e. the phenomenon that certain teachings involve objective problems which had not been realized by their originators but were detected later. More significant is the danger of even distorting the 'spirit' of a teaching or the attitude of a thinker because originally adopted views entail the irrelevance of problems highlighted in a subsequent tradition. This problem does not amount to a merely theoretical possibility. If it is true that the founder of the Madhyamaka-school advocated the non-existence of all physical and mental entities on a level of ultimate truth, he accepted a tenet suggesting an outlook according to which any attempt to *explain* the nature of illusion or the possibility of the occurrence of acts of illusion (given that they are themselves merely illusory) must amount to a futile enterprise impeding the attainment of salvation. — It should be plain that only the methodological point of the threat of underestimating the fallibility of interpreting doctrines against the background of later developments matters in the present context so that here the question as to whether the envisaged interpretation of the original Madhyamaka-teaching is correct possesses at most secondary importance.

63 Due to the apprehension that too undifferentiated views on not unimportant general issues could still be accepted it has been preferred to even bring up matters which could be taken for granted in other circumstances.

philosophy has been added not merely in order to complement criticisms presented in the first essay. It should demonstrate that the preceding discussions are suited as a starting point leading to deeper theoretical contemplations. Furthermore, the explorations in this section are geared to clarifying the roots of particular, presumably quite wide-spread, preconceptions and prejudices and should thereby help for structuring and evaluating controversies in general.

As it is a central purpose of the present treatise to evaluate by contrast the three above depicted approaches in particular and to promote the appreciation of explorations not confined to the ascertainment of historical facts in general, it can hardly suffice to merely characterize pertinent varieties without reflecting on their possible relevance. A reason for granting room for a short exposition of some issues of truth paradoxes in the first chapter of the present essay, although the topic has been investigated in the previous part, lies in the aspiration to make the potential relevance of type C-investigations more transparent. If, by touching on issues of truth and meaning in different contexts and in various ways, the subsequent presentations work up an interest in these notions among scholars studying intellectual traditions, and if they promote the readiness to acknowledge that the relationship between them possess significance for the humanities in general, this effect should be welcomed.

The Delusions of 'Historical Interpretation'

Abstract

Primary purposes of the present treatise are: 1) to show that detailed textual investigations where focus on historical connections is replaced by focus on conceptual and theoretical relations and where understandings of later interpreters need not be (explicitly) thematised are not only legitimate, but also unduly neglected and needed at present; 2) to disclose that arguments against this view, which might find wider approval than they deserve, are faulty and deserve to be rejected; 3) to corroborate these tenets by displaying the need to distinguish between different approaches of assessing philosophical traditions and highlighting some disregarded consequences entailed by this distinction. A secondary aim lies in displaying on the basis of not only empirical but also theoretical and methodological considerations the absolute untenability of a contention intimated by the title of a recently published paper claiming a final verdict concerning a debated issue in the area of theoretical Indian philosophy and to employ various details of that article for the illustration of relevant general points. The most overarching objective is however to cast doubts on the opinion that, since one has to deal with a philosophical tradition under the aspect of 'history of ideas', or '*Geistesgeschichte*', one can dispense with the need to strive after a deeper understanding of the concerned theoretical subject matter — an understanding which does not merely mirror the understanding of the writer of some textual source — and to criticize a practice harmonizing with that belief.

I

It can be tiresome to have to write on issues which have been discussed a number of times before. However, a recent paper published by E. Franco (F) on the so-called *Sadvitīyaprayoga* (SP) titled 'Final Notes on the *Sadvitīyaprayoga*' (FN)[64] has shifted the focus from the SP, which was the original topic, to matters of methodology. The circumstance that the article exhibits both a failure of understanding a criticized position as well as a significant discrepancy between apodictic claims and substantial support is not the only thing which matters. Decisively more important are a) that several fallacies which do not specifically affect discussions about the SP could remain unnoticed due to more prevalent misconceptions about the role historical considerations are able to play in principle, b) that the issues which are at stake concern studies of texts and traditions in general and that a disentanglement of truths and untruths in this matter appears to be needed, c) that certain highly questionable tenets concerning the appropriate way of dealing with philosophical traditions suggested in FN are equally intimated in articles written by other authors and d) that F defends his case in an unacceptably irresponsible manner by undermining vital ingredients of scientific integrity. This has created a situation which makes a rigorous contestation unavoidable. All the main points expounded below possess implications which definitely transcend the topic of the SP.

It deserves to be made clear from the outset that, as far as the SP is concerned, no contention exists on my part to the effect that some particular interpretation, advocated by me, can claim exclusive legitimacy. It is precisely a major purpose of the subsequent exposition to indicate that and why on account of principal theoretical reasons *nobody* could maintain such a prerogative not

64 *Journal of Indian Philosophy* (2016) 44:525–535. Published online: 16 May 2015. DOI 10.1007/s10781-015-9273-8.

only in the case of the SP but also in all other cases which are similar.[65] What will be attempted to show, however, is that important matters threaten to fall into oblivion, if a critical inspection of various issues which are brought up in FN were omitted. For the primary problem is not due to the mere circumstance that this essay exhibits various pieces of reasoning not complying with standards of strictness required for acceptable solutions of questions even in the area of traditional philologies. Decisively more important is the fact that *de facto* — whether intended or not, can be left open — FN amounts to an attempt to discredit the insistence on more

[65] In view of the possible allegation that the thesis suffers from insufficient novelty because it could be regarded as a version of the renowned doctrine of the under-determination of theories by data the following points deserve to be remarked: First, something which could be regarded as a truism by certain philosophers is not necessarily a commonplace for everyone. Second, advocating some theorem on the one hand and illustrating that and why some version of it holds true in some particular area on the other hand are different matters. Third, the sort of indeterminateness which possesses primary relevance in the present connection is *not* the same as the indeterminacy pertaining to the interpretation of a language; it mostly arises due to contingent circumstances and affects the interpretation of linguistic tokens and not of types as elements of a linguistic system. Accordingly it is on the one hand theoretically less fundamental but on the other hand practically more relevant than the sorts of underdetermination discussed in the context of linguistics and philosophy. Fourth, the pertinent view is connected with tenets concerning meaning and content which are by no means commonly acknowledged, in particular the theses that different types of meaning and content exist and that textual exegesis is regularly concerned with types of meaning and content which are most crucially underdetermined by available data. Although those matters are not the primary topic here, it is apposite to at least bring them up at this point. They are, among others, important for recognizing the crudeness of FN's rhetorical question (p. 534) as to how it is possible to 'understand' something's 'meaning without considering it in its historical context'. The truth is rather that the identification of *particular types* of meaning or content requires considerations of (certain varieties and features of) context. Last but not least, it is quite astonishing that someone who ought to have heard of the thesis that there are different sorts of understanding with respect to linguistic and related items completely ignores this tenet or takes its falsity simply for granted without argument.

demanding standards of rigor, and it is this precarious peculiarity which explains the focusing on FN for purposes of illustration.

II

The main points are as follows:

1.

It is true that the tenet is supported by me that at present an urgent need exists to complement studies dealing with historical developments in the area of Indian (and presumably also other non-Western) philosophies by detailed enquiries concerning individual texts and textual passages and that investigations of this sort do not *need* to make sources belonging to later historical periods a subject of discussion — which does not rule out that their knowledge is implicitly taken into consideration. The postulate is based on the view that textual analysis calls for a degree of depth and intensity which is not achieved by merely historically oriented studies and surveys. It is a major mistake to claim that this manner of excluding the history of reception makes matters of textual exegesis arbitrary. There are different criteria which restrict the acceptability of interpretations in the area of theoretical treatises. They can be subdivided into three main subcategories, viz.

(a) grammatical criteria
(b) pragmatic criteria
(c) theoretical criteria.

Among those

(a) relates to rules valid for specific natural languages as well as conventions generally obeyed in some linguistic community.[66]

[66] This provides the foundation for a kind of understanding which can be achieved even with respect to isolated sentences or constituents of possible sentences occurring e.g. in the form of quoted examples in the context of

It is to be noted that, although the circumstance that some interpretation implies a violation of such rules or conventions generally diminishes the probability of its correctness to a significant degree, it is in the first place the indisputable occurrence of failures of linguistic performance which forbids to consider this criterion as absolutely decisive.

(b) comprises (at least) two components, viz. (i) maximal suitability of some existing formulation to be interpreted for the communicative goals implied by the hypothesized interpretation or exegesis and (ii) intra-textual context, sometimes designated by the technical term 'co-text'. Due to (i) the mere circumstance that relative to an existing formulation an alternative exists which would be better suited for the realization of the hypothesized communicative goals provides a relevant reason for decreasing the acceptability of an interpretation.[67] As far as (ii) is concerned, (by default) primary relevance needs to be attributed to the preceding co-text in comparison to the subsequent co-text as well as to other textual passages written by an identical author.[68] The reason is that

linguistic studies. For this sort of understanding it is immaterial whether or not the pertinent expressions contain indexical elements as constituents. On the other hand it yields a valid basis for assessing what a competent user of an expression could, and presumably will, but not must (!), mean under possible circumstances.

[67] It must be admitted that if languages come into play which are not native tongues of an interpreter this methodological tool tends to become less powerful. But precisely this circumstance sustains the contention that even for a classical philologist acquisition of a certain amount of active competence in a foreign language possesses relevance.

[68] It can be presumed that neglect of this point arises out of a failure to clearly and consistently discriminate between two different tasks (corresponding with two separate senses of the expression 'mean'), namely i) the task of ascertaining communicative intentions connected with particular utterances on the one hand and ii) the task of identifying pertinent totalities of beliefs held by an individual speakeror author on the other. — The principle of the priority of preceding over subsequent co-text must surely not be taken in an excessively restricted manner so that it would militate against the fact that the

somebody who writes a text usually attempts to practice a linguistic behaviour which (as far as possible) enables potential addressees to correctly grasp his communicative intentions without having to rely on information not provided before.[69]

(c) encompasses (at least) the following two elements: (i) The theoretical situation at the time in which some textual passage has been written, (ii) the objective theoretical tenability and significance. (i) is pertinent for diminishing the peril of accepting 'anachronistic' interpretations. Usually (but not necessarily always!) the plausibility of an interpretation is

question of the — pragmatic or pragmatic and theoretical — relevance of immediately subsequent remarks can sometimes provide a most important methodological tool for the determination of the import of some earlier linguistic unit. To some extent the producer of a sequence of utterances can legitimately demand and expect that addressees will be disposed to revisit and reconsider his remarks, and this holds good in particular, if acts of communication take place in the written medium. Thus in the final analysis the most decisive criterion lies in the possibility to preserve the presumption that a speaker or writer exhibits an adequate linguistic behavior.

69 Considering the fact that linguistic formulations often do not reveal by themselves the topic of the context of their occurrence, the priority of previous co-text attains special significance whenever textual sources are concerned which deal with a multitude of topics, as e.g. the *Nyāyasūtra*s: It is the immediately preceding co-text in particular which should provide clues for the identification of the pertinent subject matter. The criterion is relevant even in cases where one must reckon with the possibility that an existent textual source contains later insertions so that its application serves the purpose of settling questions concerning the import envisaged by the subject who inserted a formulation, whereas questions concerning the import intended by its original creator would need to refer to different criteria, such as details of formulation. It is even conceivable that the criterion attains relevance in the field of textual criticism: If in an existing version of a text a passage occurs implying a substantial determination (not necessarily distortion) of the meaning of some fairly distant preceding segment, this fact can provide a clue for the identification of later insertions. — One must not misunderstand those statements as militating against the possibility that a writer, realizing that he had not expressed himself with sufficient clarity before, adds clarifying remarks later, maybe even in the form of another work.

enhanced by the circumstance that it helps to explain *why* some writer has said something by showing that he can have considered his saying as relevant in some socio-historical context.[70] (ii) possesses significance not only due to the fact that if an interpretation entails the attribution of blatant errors it deserves to be met with scepticism, but also because fairness to a tradition and its representatives demands that one looks for the theoretically most insightful stance compatible with the criteria of the categories (a) and(b).[71]

In contrast to the aforementioned aspects consideration of how a textual passage or theorem has been understood by later interpreters can only possess a heuristic significance. The reason should be patent: Other person's *beliefs* of what something means or somebody else has meant are principally unsuited as a *criterion* for supporting or even deciding what something or someone actually means. The opposite view contradicts the sound intuition that there is neither an entailment

---

70 Strictly speaking there is an overlap between the categories (b) and (c) in this regard.

71 Those criteria come into play for the derivation of some content from a linguistic formulation. Once a content is established as being supported by relevant criteria, one can pose questions of a different sort pertaining to objective properties of the content in question, such as what is entailed by it, what is incompatible with it, what would be probable or improbable if it represented a truth, which theoretical position is supported, refuted or called into question etc. Issues of the latter type are relevant for the assessment of the theoretical significance of theorems or arguments like the SP. One cannot attribute much value to any criticism which, instead of keeping clearly apart the different components pertinent for the subject matter, muddles them up. — It is a well-known fact that, as a rule, human beings do not recognize all properties of abstract objects and, in particular, everything which is objectively implied by some content. Moreover, something which one subject perceives as a consequence need not be discerned by others too. Hence — pace F and FN — the mere circumstance that certain textual sources do not exhibit an awareness of particular consequences implied by some content or theoretical item cannot disprove the supposition that ideas entailing the pertinent consequences might be much older than the sources in question.

between being true and being believed to be true nor between being believed to be true and being in fact true.[72]

To be sure, it is not seldom impossible to employ the above portrayed criteria for uniquely determining some particular interpretation. This problem is particularly virulent in the case of the SP where one cannot even rely on criteria of co-text. But it is nothing else than a matter of fidelity to clearly acknowledge indeterminateness instead of feigning decidability by (mis)using the authority of opinions held in some later tradition. To be sure, precisely the frequent under-determination of meaning by linguistic rules and knowledge about context bestows a certain amount of relevance of taking into account how something has been understood in a tradition of later interpreters. This relevance is nonetheless of a purely heuristic nature: It derives from the fact that taking opinions into account can assist us in recognizing possibilities of interpretation which otherwise could be easily overlooked. The importance of paying attention to traditions of exegesis could be somewhat higher if it presented not only opinions but also reasons for the concerned opinions. But even under such circumstances the mere fact that opinions have been accompanied by reasons cannot license definite verdicts about interpretations. It is mandatory to first assess the validity of the reasons themselves so that in any case the role of considering traditions of interpretation remains heuristic: Its relevance is rooted in the fact that it potentially diminishes the danger of neglecting reasons which can be pertinent for making decisions in matters of interpretation. Hence for vindicating that a tradition of exegesis has been unduly neglected it would be necessary to show that either

72 Against this one cannot validly object that a belief can serve as a criterion whenever its very existence is due to the circumstance that its content represents a fact. In such special cases it is strictly speaking not the belief itself which could function as a criterion but only the combination of the existence of the belief plus the circumstance that the truth of its content provides the only plausible explanation of its existence.

specific significant possibilities of interpretation or relevant reasons for deciding exegetical issues have been disregarded due to such neglect.

F's paper does not only fail to give evidence for any presentation of exegetical reasons in the tradition subsequent to the first presentation of the SP, but it also omits the chance of introducing a slightly higher degree of sophistication and differentiation into the discussion by drawing attention to the above-mentioned difference. This is surely deplorable. One must moreover regret that the article completely ignores the question whether it can be expected that later interpreters criticizing the SP intended to do justice to it. My own surmise — which had been expressed earlier — is that this expectation must not be taken for granted. Therefore the position which appears to be advocated in FN is not only fallacious, but potentially pernicious: It invites one to practice unfairness to individual writers and works by too uncritically accepting verdicts of persons who intended to criticize them.

For demonstrating that the surmise that later critics failed to do justice to the SP is more than an empty speculation, a brief inspection of Dharmakīrti's criticism in the *Pramāṇavārttika* (PV) IV, 34–39, taking into account remarks in the *Pramāṇaviniścaya* (PVin), another work of the same author, suffices. The vital feature of the criticism lies in rejecting as sufficient for the validity and acceptability of an argument a compliance with the requirements a) that a quality employed as a reason = *probans* (or *hetu*) is in fact exhibited by a substratum of inference = *pakṣa* and b) that in the domain outside the *pakṣa* it holds unfailingly true that everything exhibiting the *probans* also exhibits the quality to be proven = the *probandum* (or *sādhya*), if the *probandum* consists in the disjunctive property of possessing as a second counterpart, i.e. differing from, either a body manifesting consciousness, i.e. a conscious body, or that which, as a matter of fact, functions as a *pakṣa*, which is in the pertinent case an individual pot or collection of pots.

In principle such a refusal could be based on the view that disjunctive qualities are generally inadmissible as *sādhya.* This is presumably not presupposed by the writer of the text. Another possibility would be an adoption of the weaker tenet that disjunctive qualities are admissible only if i) at least one object instantiates all the members of the disjunction or ii) all members of the disjunction are instantiated by at least one item, such that the fact of their instantiation is indisputable.[73] No matter whether or not Dharmakīrti accepted these propositions, any criticism which vitally depends on such a questionable premise can hardly do justice to the SP.[74] A further possible basis can lie in the consideration that a hypothetically assumed proponent employing the SP would, by employing the argument, intend to establish the contention that material bodies as substrata of consciousness exist. In that case the refutation of the SP would crucially depend on the supposition that users of the SP must be materialists and that the only (realistically) conceivable function of the SP lies in

[73] To be sure, the SP relies on a dismissal of this demand, but there is no sound reason to regard this circumstance as fatal for the SP-argument.

[74] Let us suppose that from some town T an older route A and a newly built route B leads to some city C and that there is no other way from T to C. Suppose further that we know that some person P will travel from T to C. Intuitively the argument: 'P will come to C either by route A or by route B because he starts from T' is stronger than the argument: 'P will come to C by route A because he starts from T'. At least one can definitely ascertain that the first reasoning is not more unsecure than the second alternative. This holds even good in a situation in which P has never travelled before from T to C on the route B and where it is doubtful whether he or anyone else will ever travel on this route to C. This shows that not only i), but even the postulate ii) is pretty implausible. It demonstrates in addition the dubiousness of the requirement of (positive) 'examples'. In this connection the circumstance attains importance that at least the argumentation of the PV could be most naturally interpreted as vitally relying on ii). — Note that ii) differs from the requirement that all members of a disjunction must represent *possibilities*, so that it needs to be both conceivable that P reaches T via A and conceivable that P reaches T via B. (We will revert to this point later).

establishing a tenet advocated by materialists.[75] Even if the assumption that the SP should be used for establishing a materialistic tenet were taken for granted, the demand that a materialist is *obliged* to prove his thesis by a form of argument in which the (non-disjunctive) quality of (something's) possessing as a counterpart a body endowed with consciousness functions as *probandum* is quite peculiar, because this is apt to provoke the question: What entitles Dharmakīrti to dictate to the materialist the manner in which he has to demonstrate the truth of his proposition? The reply that Dharmakīrti's own theoretical outlook does not allow for any alternative way is hardly convincing. In this case the materialist could confront the author of the PV with the answer: 'All the worse for your philosophical theory!'

A most interesting possibility of criticism is provided by a crucial feature of the SP which the author of the PV (and of the PVin) could have exploited and (implicitly) recognized: The reason why the exhibition of the disjunctive property is guaranteed in the domain apart from the subject of proof (the *pakṣa*) lies precisely in the fact that the items belonging to that domain are different from it; all (existing) items which differ from the *pakṣa* exhibit the property of having a pot (functioning as *pakṣa*) as a different counterpart and thereby exemplify the disjunctive quality of having either a pot or a conscious body as a counterpart exactly because they do not belong to the domain of the *pakṣa*.[76] Hence an *anvaya* restricted to the domain outside the *pakṣa* can exist only for that reason. It is nothing else than this fact which forbids the transfer or extrapolation of a feature

---

[75] These are, as a matter of fact, questionable presuppositions. Since this issue will be addressed later it is not further explored in the present context.

[76] This is not a consideration explicitly expressed in the PV (or the PVin) but a fact which is exploited for the purpose of criticism, particularly by the — interesting but unconvincing — argument that, given that the existence of conscious bodies is a matter of doubt, no example conclusively establishes the connection between the *probans* and the disjunctive *probandum* by exemplifying one member of the disjunction which could be equally exemplified by the substratum of inference, i.e. the *pakṣa*.

exhibited in the entire non-*pakṣa* realm to the *pakṣa* itself. But by exploiting this peculiarity for criticizing the SP Dharmakīrti misrepresents its significance which consists in the following problem: How can we be assured that it is not the case that a regularity in some domain holds unfailingly good only because the domain in question differs from another domain? How can we be confident that even if we possess strong evidence for an unviolated regularity in a particular realm we do not go astray if we infer some fact in a way whose validity crucially depends on the premise that the same regularity holds good in a different realm or under different circumstances? What guarantees, for example, that law-like regularities which are in fact never violated in situations where the relative movement of different bodies is relatively low cannot be violated in situations where the velocity of movements is extremely high, or that dispositions always exhibited by certain kinds of objects under conditions of normal temperature are also exhibited by objects in situations of extreme heat or extreme cold? The problem which is at stake does not merely concern the application of a law-hypothesis to novel instances but the possibility of extrapolating law-like connections themselves to different kinds of situations. It is a problem which vitally affects Dharmakīrti's idea of *svabhāvapratibandha* and the role which can be attributed to it.[77] The crux is that the relevance

[77] As far as one can see, Dharmakīrti has never discriminated the idea of an absolute relation of cause and effect, represented by propositions of the form 'A is cause of B' or 'A-s are causes of B-s', from relativized concepts of cause-effect relation, represented by propositions of the form 'Under the circumstance C, an A causes B' or 'In the situation S A functions as a cause of B'. This is relevant in so far as any demonstration to the effect that it can be definitely established by some test that in particular (sorts of) situations some specific feature, such as the occurrence of fire, functions as a causally relevant (and indispensable) factor for the occurrence of some (kind of) event, such as occurrence of smoke, does not *eo ipso* vindicate the contention that there is a possibility to establish in a categorical form that the existence of the concerned feature is always a necessary prerequisite for the existence of the pertinent event so that one can safely infer on the basis of a perception of smoke that some fire occurs somewhere. By seeing this matter clearly one is

of a framework condition must not be always immediately obvious.[78] It is not justified to argue that the possible circumstance that in the tradition of Dharmakīrti neither this problem nor its derivability from the SP has been articulated establishes that the problem does not exist and that one cannot legitimately distil it from the SP. This is as if one would contend that the circumstance that a contradiction in a mathematical theory has not been detected (up to a specific time) establishes that it does not exist.[79]

There are also other regards in which the account presented in the PV (and elsewhere) fails to throw into relief vital aspects of the theoretical significance of the SP, if it (viz. the formulation of the SP) is interpreted in accordance with (c)(ii): A derivation of the pertinent 'materialist' tenet would involve *two* components. The first step consists in the establishment of the exemplification of a disjunctive quality in accordance with criteria of *anumāna*. The second step consists in the elimination of the possibility that some particular item exemplifies one of the disjuncts, and the validity of this step is *not* a matter of complying with such criteria, specifically the criteria stipulated in the doctrine of *trairūpya*, but possesses entirely different

enabled to recognize that inferences based on hypotheses of causal relations are always by nature probabilistic. It is the formal property of 'If P, then if/whenever A then B' which furnishes a relevant link between invariable regularities like in the case of the SP on the one hand and the idea of domain-specific causal connections on the other; in the first case 'P' is replaceable by expressions such as: 'If something is not the *pakṣa*' and in the latter case by expressions, such as: 'If a temperature above X degrees prevails' etc. By failing to distil this abstract feature Dharmakīrti missed an opportunity to inspect his own outlook with a more critical eye.

78 Therefore a significant issue is the question as to whether such a theory could ever be suited in areas such as linguistics or economics.

79 One wonders, by the way, whether the recommendations advocated in FN imply that, instead of investigating a mathematical theory itself, one must first of all examine whether the existence of a contradiction has been asserted in sources representing the mathematical tradition of the subsequent ten, fifty or hundred years. — Anyhow, the objection that examination of the tradition can be important as an aid for finding out the truth of the matter rests again on a confusion between heuristic devices and criteria.

theoretical roots. In this regard the SP transcends the framework of theories of 'means of valid knowledge' (*pramāṇa*), in particular the version which is adopted by the author of the text.

The SP can be most naturally integrated in an argumentative context directed against a theory or against proponents of a theory supposing that certainty concerning the impossibility of the occurrence of a *probans* without the *probandum* in some (large) domain licenses the presumption of the same regularity in any (smaller and) specific domain. Such an argument could run as follows:

> It is assumed (by you) that the following principle is valid: Whenever we are (absolutely) certain that in the whole domain which remains, if we disregard some specific object or realm of objects (about which we desire to know more), it holds good that everything which exhibits some feature H also exhibits some particular feature S, then we are entitled to derive that objects belonging to the specific domain will exhibit S, given that they exhibit H. But let us consider any of the following pieces of reasoning:
>
> > 'The pot (which is in front of us) is such that it either numerically differs from this pot (which is in front of us) or numerically differs from at least one conscious material body because it is not a lotus, as e.g. a wall'
>
> or:
>
> > 'The collection of all pots (of the world) is such that each element either numerically differs from all pots (of the world) or from at least one material body which is a substratum of consciousness because it is (such that each of its elements is) not a lotus, as e.g. a wall.'
>
> In both cases we can be absolutely certain that in the non-specific realm all items exhibiting the probans (H) must also exhibit the probandum (S). However, (given that the pertinent principle is

truth-preserving and thus) supposing that this circumstance guarantees the truth of the pertinent conclusion it follows that the proposition that the pot which is in front of us differs either from itself or from at least one conscious material body, or, alternatively, the proposition that every pot either differs from every pot (including itself) or from at least one conscious material body, needs to represent a truth. But a possibility of preserving truth could only exist if pots numerically differ from conscious material bodies, which means that (at least some) material body which is a substratum of consciousness must exist. This is surely not something which you (or we) want to accept.

The crucial point is that according to this reconstruction the primarily derived consequence is *not* the existence of conscious bodies but the corollary that pots are such that they *either* differ from themselves *or* from some conscious body. Since this proposition is at least a *possible* truth one cannot simply discard the relevance of the argument by stipulating that a piece of reasoning must not attempt to establish a thesis whose falsity is indisputable.[80] The crucial point is rather that a possible truth is derived that itself implies consequences which are regarded as unacceptable by certain persons and that for those who regard the entailed corollary as true a parallel argument can be construed simply by replacing 'is different from' by 'is never different from' possessing an implication which they could not accept as true.

Against this background the objective need not to be seen in the establishment of some or the other 'metaphysical' tenet but in the demonstration of the fallacious nature of a certain principle of reasoning. The decisive point is the following: It is not the case that that which appears *within* the SP as a thesis, or technically as *pratijñā*,

---

80 Precisely the *combination* of the features of being necessarily satisfied by all items in the domain outside the *pakṣa* (and specifically in the subsection of that domain where the *probans* is instantiated) and of being possibly, i.e. conceivably, satisfied by the *pakṣa* (or by items constituting the realm of the *pakṣa*) bestows on the *sādhya*-predicate the peculiar character which is responsible for the significance of the SP.

is meant to be established as true by that which appears as a reason, or technically as a *hetu*. Rather the entire reasoning (consisting of *pratijñā, hetu* and *dṛṣṭānta*) is presented as an example (in the usual sense, and not in the technical sense of the term *dṛṣṭānta*), so that the presentation *as a whole* should demonstrate the vulnerability of particular standards of inferential reasoning, and this contention is established in a fairly convincing manner. Under these circumstances it would be inappropriate to characterize the argument as a 'sophism' in any defensible sense of the word. To be sure, the writer of the PV does obviously not consider the SP under this perspective. But one should be entitled to ask: Was he (or F) justified to neglect this aspect of the matter?

Under the perspective of cross-cultural comparison, the fact that the SP appears to exploit a familiar logical intuition can prove to be significant: It is the intuition which lies behind a renowned rule designated by the terms 'disjunction introduction', 'disjunction addition' or 'or-introduction' and which licences the derivation of any disjunctive proposition of the form 'P or Q' from a proposition 'P' as an assumption. With respect to the realm of predicates the same intuition supports the view that if some predicate 'Fx' is true of some object then a disjunctive predicate of the form 'Fx or Gx' must equally be true of the same object, no matter what 'Gx' stands for. It is by no means eccentric to suppose that the proponent(s) of the SP were guided by similar intuitions and implicitly acknowledged rules which are fairly familiar to us. Hence there is an objective reason which *could* have caused the author of the PV and the PVin to raise the question of the legitimacy of the concerned intuitions and of the validity of the corresponding rules or theorems in a general and explicit form. This has, however, not happened and, presumably, did not happen in the tradition after Dharmakīrti either. If that is true, a phenomenon of absence can be ascertained whose dismissal as insignificant even under the aspect of intellectual history or *Geistesgeschichte* would require quite a narrow(-minded) view on the matter. On the other hand it is true that certain remarks made by the writer of the PVin intimate an implicit rejection or at least reservations regarding the principle of disjunction addition. Those are, however, presumably based on considerations pertaining to the *appropriateness of using* disjunctive sentences or predicates rather than on facts relating to properties of their (semantic) contents and are in this manner reminiscent of the phenomenon that expressions of the form 'It is possible that P or Q' are commonly employed and understood in the sense of 'It is possible that P and it is possible that Q' in contrast to a theorem acknowledged in various systems of Modal Logic, according to which expressions of the first form are equivalent to expressions of the form 'It is possible that P or it is possible that Q'.

With respect to Dharmakīrti's philosophy in particular, the critical potential that inheres in the SP could be depicted as follows:

> It might be granted that, *if* there are essential connections in the sense of *svabhāvapratibandha*, *then* secure inferences transferring state-of-affairs from some (previously explored) realm to a different (not explored) realm, must be possible, at least in theory. But the crucial problem lies in the question as to how it can be vindicated that essential connections in the pertinent sense really exist.

It is neither necessary nor appropriate to go deeper into details here, because in the present context only the following observations matter: 1) Given that the above portrayed questions and problems are not explicitly articulated in textual sources representing the history of reception of the SP, they cannot be discerned and assessed merely on the basis of taking specimens of its criticism into consideration, but require analyses which go decisively beyond those which are exemplified by current varieties of text-interpretation in the framework of historical studies. 2) Nobody who wants to ensure that the future tradition of study of Indian philosophies will not persist in a state of inferiority relative to other disciplines can permit that F's contentions in FN furnish a sufficient motivation for discarding the legitimacy of problem-oriented explorations in the field.

Recognition of the above ascertained facts is not provided by a verbal understanding of a textual passage representing a criticism of the SP (an understanding which is required for achieving an acceptable translation) but only by a theoretical understanding of a pertinent subject matter, which is an entirely different, and in some regards more demanding type of understanding. This is comparable with the understanding of a mathematical proof, something which is not ensured by either perceptual understanding (recognition of sounds or graphic symbols) or verbal understanding (understanding of the meaning of expressions, in particular the words employed by somebody who presents a proof). It is perhaps the combination of propagating verbal understanding and simultaneously discrediting theoretical understanding which represents one of the most perverted ingredients of FN.[81] One ought to note in addition that the pertinent passage of the PV does not offer relevant help for a better *verbal* understanding of the SP.

The preceding remarks must not be taken as entailing an absolute separation between the levels of verbal and theoretical understanding in the sense that any form of interdependency, and

[81] The above presented exposition intimates that the reception of theoretical items in a tradition can be an interesting topic of study. Hence one should have agreed to F if he had confined himself to asserting that this subject matter should not be neglected. What deserves strong opposition are however F's apodictic claims concerning the necessity to bring opinions of later interpreters into play irrespective of the context and the aims of an investigation. What matters most in the final analysis is not how many but *how* primary or secondary sources are read. (There is a certain parallelism with the priority of 'internal understanding' in the field of arts: Knowing that a certain sequence of intervals in a theme of a Beethoven sonata equally occurs in some work of Wagner must not contribute to a better interpretation of the sonata; rather the contrary could be an outcome).

in particular dependence of (understanding of) meaning on (understanding of) theory (even in a narrow sense of the term 'theory'), is precluded. Despite the emphasis on the difference, the possibility should be admitted that theories can determine the meaning of terms in more than one sense of the word 'determine'. They should in particular permit us to subscribe to the tenet that 'understanding the technical language of a subject requires that we understand its theories, and to understand its theories we need to understand the language' and that 'we understand both by looking for the problems which the theories solve by using' a 'modified language'.[82]

Although in the present connection it is not intended to go deeper into the concerned questions of linguistic change and innovation, it ought to be pointed out that they possess relevance for some more general aspects of the criticism put forward in the following section, in particular the problem of extrapolating semantic assessments concerning linguistic tokens from certain contexts to others.

FN does not submit a single argument against the contentions 1) that detailed textual investigations not aiming at describing historical developments are needed at present and 2) that the — one should think elementary — distinction between criteria and heuristic devices cannot be ignored. The article does not even reveal the slightest awareness of those points. Thus the most plausible conclusion is that its author has not adequately understood the position he attempts to criticize.

2.

The first contention, viz. the relevance of investigating immanent properties of individual textual passages and of respecting individual characteristics, can be substantiated by taking a closer look at the issue which, according to the abstract of FN, constitutes the second major

[82] Cf. Hattiangadi 1987:12. In the present connection it is legitimate and even appropriate to abstain from discussing the question whether (perhaps not unimportant) additions would be needed to account for the circumstance that linguistic change and innovation as well as significance for language learning do not exclusively pertain to declarative sentences.

topic of that article, in particular at the way in which F argues for the affirmation that the expressions *sapakṣa* and *vipakṣa* must be interpreted as 'collective terms'. This thesis is combined with the claim that those words have to be rendered with definite articles. First, the argument offered in FN to the effect that '[i]f the word *vipakṣa* were not used as a collective term, the formulation *vipakṣe 'sattvam* would not be adequate because it would leave open the possibility that the reason exists in another *vipakṣa*' (p. 532) is pretty useless. This is because an indefinite noun phrase in the singular can easily be used for conveying a universally quantified proposition, as evidenced by

> In a Swedish supermarket there is no alcohol to be sold.
> In einem schwedischen Supermarkt kann man keinen Alkohol bekommen.

etc.[83] It is instructive to consider the pertinent issue against the background of an example. In the well-known *Nyāyapraveśa* the following passage occurs:

---

[83] It remains, moreover, unclear, why the same ambiguity should not exist if the expression *vipakṣe* (in formulations without *eva*) refers to collections, groups or realms of particulars. It deserves to be equally noted in passing that F's contention (FN, p. 532) to the effect that in the terms *sapakṣaikadeśavṛtti* and *vipakṣaikadeśavṛtti* the constituents *sapakṣa*- and *vipakṣa*- must be understood as referring to an entire domain is doubtful. The reason is that in non-final members of compounds markers of number (singular, dual or plural) do not occur so that the conclusion that their compositional sense amounts to 'presence in a part of (the domain of) *sapakṣa/vipakṣa'* is not compelling. One can say, either

> The sabre-toothed tiger is extinct.
> Die Säbelzahnkatze ist ausgestorben.

or

> Sabre-toothed tigers are extinct.
> Säbelzahnkatzen sind ausgestorben.

Similarly, one could attribute to the expressions *sapakṣaikadeśavṛtti* and *vipakṣaikadeśavṛtti* as compositional meanings 'presence in a part of the *sapakṣas*' and 'presence in a part of the *vipakṣas*' — or, supposing that the surface-forms are not fully explicit, 'occurrence at one [particular] place [in

> *hetus trirūpaḥ* | *kiṃ punas trairūpyam* | *pakṣadharmatvaṃ sapakṣe sattvaṃ vipakṣe cāsattvam iti* || *kaḥ punaḥ sapakṣaḥ* | *ko vā vipakṣa iti* || ***sādhyadharmasāmānyena samāno 'rthaḥ sapakṣaḥ*** | ***tad yathā*** | ***anitye śabde sādhye ghaṭādir anityaḥ sapakṣaḥ*** || *vipakṣo yatra sādhyaṃ nāsti* | *yan nityaṃ tad akṛtakaṃ dṛṣṭaṃ yathākāśam iti* | ***tatra kṛtakatvaṃ prayatnānantarīyakatvaṃ vā sapakṣa evāsti vipakṣe nāsty eva*** | *ity anityādau hetuḥ* ||
> (page 1,8 in the edition of A.B. Dhruva 1968)

Here the most relevant segments are written in bold and can be rendered as follows:

> ("But what is *sapakṣa*? Or what is *vipakṣa*?") *Sapakṣa* is a thing which is similar by the similarity of the *dharma* [which is] to be proven.[84] For example: If sound has to be proven as non-eternal the non-eternal pot etc. is *sapakṣa*. .... (Since) therefore producedness or [the quality of] ensuing upon effort is only in *sapakṣa* and never in *vipakṣa* (it is a correct reason with respect to [something's being] impermanent etc.).

A most natural reading of the first segment containing the explanation of *sapakṣa* suggests a concept according to which (being) *sapakṣa* characterizes individual objects, like pots, which are non-eternal.[85] —

---

the domain of] *sapakṣas*'. For ruling out this alternative possibility and vindicating F's contention one would need to rely on the claim that the pertinent expressions can *never* be used in the sense of nouns in the plural. Even admitting that textual evidence establishes that *sapakṣa-* and *vipakṣa-* *can* occur in the singular or even supposing that they ordinarily appear as singular nouns, it is questionable that pieces of textual evidence can license such far-reaching conclusions about linguistic possibilities. One ought to relentlessly insist on the postulate of a willingness to reflect upon those matters irrespective of the question as to what conception individual people might have regarding the character of their discipline.

84 Or: 'A thing which .... , is (a) *sapakṣa*'.

85 The situation would be completely different if the text would read: *sādhyadharmasāmānyena samānā arthāḥ sapakṣaḥ*. In this case, it would be most natural to interpret the sentence in the sense of: '[The collection of all] the objects which are similar by the similarity of the *dharma* [which is] to be

This means that *sapakṣa* can occur in the syntactic position of a predicate meaning 'is a *sapakṣa'*. — A similar interpretation is possible (though not mandatory) regarding the remarks that producedness etc. is only in *sapakṣa* and that *vipakṣa* is (something) where the quality to be proven never exists (or occurs). — Even if the words occur as nouns here, they are equivalent to 'that which is a *sapakṣa/vipakṣa*'. — On the other hand the last two remarks can (perhaps) be most easily brought in line with the idea that the expressions designate groups or realms of particular objects.[86] But, even if this contention would be granted, one should be entitled to pose the question: Why is it imperative to assimilate either the reading of the first segment to the perhaps most natural reading of the second segment or the reading of the second segment to the most natural reading of the first? Why is it compulsory to posit any homogenization at all instead of admitting that the manner of employing the words is not uniform and that the most natural readings are to be accepted in all

---

proven are/constitute the *sapakṣa*' or: 'The *sapakṣa* is/is constituted by (all) the objects which ....'. But precisely this wording is not found in the text. Although F, in FN p. 532, refers to the *Nyāyapraveśa*, he writes as if he had not critically read the pertinent textual source.

86 Nonetheless, it is important to pay due attention to the circumstance that the phrase *sapakṣa evāsti vipakṣe nāsty eva* can be consistently interpreted in the sense of: 'occurs only in a *sapakṣa* (= in something which is a *sapakṣa*) and does exclusively not occur in a *vipakṣa* (= never occurs in something which is a *vipakṣa*)'. The mere *possibility* to obtain an acceptable interpretation of the entire sentence also on the basis of a 'collective interpretation' of the word(-token)s *sapakṣ[e]* and *vipakṣe* can merely yield a fallacious argument for the necessity of this reading, because it is not an uncommon phenomenon that differences on some lower syntactic level are 'neutralized' on some higher level. This can not only be caused by particular features exhibited by the content of the context in which an expression is embedded but can also be due to the circumstance that one and the same surface-structure masks differences on some deeper underlying level. It seems that at least in the field of Sanskrit philology a widespread ignorance or neglect of the latter possibility, which provides, among others, an explanation for the neutralization between 'and' and 'or' or its equivalents of other languages in various contexts, still constitutes a major methodological shortcoming.

cases? If however even within a single textual passage there is no need to hypothesize a completely uniform and consistent manner of using expressions there should be even less reason to dogmatically presuppose that the employments of the expressions *sapakṣa* and *vipakṣa* are exactly identical in all texts and contexts.[87]

As a matter of fact, F spends much energy in establishing that a considerable number of authors employed the pertinent terms as devices for the designation of 'groups' or 'classes'. There is not the slightest need to dispute any of those claims themselves. For the decisive aspect of the matter lies in the query of what follows from the (hypothetical) supposition that all those claims are correct. To be sure, a relevant implication *would* exist if it could be taken for granted that the expressions must *always* be used in exactly the same way. But one has to fear that the underlying principle of imposing readings on textual passages from other passages is the outcome of a crucial lack of reflection on matters of linguistic practice.[88] An uncritical acceptance of the principle cannot be excused by the allegation that it corresponds to a common practice among scholars. For this circumstance would make the situation even worse. On the other hand, it appears to be a fairly widespread feature of natural languages that the same linguistic items which can designate individuals can also designate groups of individuals, and that terms used in certain contexts for denoting species, genera or types are used in other contexts for referring to particulars,

[87] It appears that F does not completely ignore the fact that different tokens of identical linguistic types can refer to different types of objects, but he does not allow that this takes effect in the framework of the pertinent topic.

[88] This possesses general importance because the distinguishing feature of a genuine science does not primarily lie in the mere presentation of reasons and arguments but rather in a basic readiness to embark on higher-order reflections concerning the validity of arguments.

individuals or tokens.[89] Not less important is the fact that the same words can occur in different syntactic positions in different contexts.[90] This observation is specifically relevant for the debated issue. First F imputes to me the thesis that 'the term *sapakṣa* must refer to an individual thing that possesses the property to be proved' (p. 531). This allegation is definitely wrong precisely because it is exactly this underlying stereotyped presupposition which is rejected by me. For a sufficiently precise account of the pertinent tenet one would need to say that it means the following: *if* one would characterize the content of a particular argument which has been termed *pakṣasapakṣānyataratva*-argument by using the expression *sapakṣa* in its formulation, *then* one cannot (or should not) use the wording: 'Sound is permanent because it is either the *pakṣa* or the *sapakṣa*' but rather 'Sound is permanent because it is either the *pakṣa* or a *sapakṣa*'. The motivation for this contention is intimately connected with the criterion of the category (c)(ii) mentioned above: Given that *sapakṣa* refers to a group or realm of objects it becomes extremely hard to reconcile the content of the argument with the assumption — advocated by F himself in an earlier article — that it complies with the second condition of the doctrine of *trairūpya*, because it is difficult to maintain the truth of the proposition that some particular permanent object is (identifiable with) the group or the realm of all items exemplifying the quality to be

[89] Interestingly F refers (p. 533) among others to a statement in Dignāga's *Nyāyamukha*, where the author seems to clarify that in characterizations of the reason and so on certain words in the singular, among them also the word *sapakṣa*, do not refer to specific individuals, but to a 'class' or a 'collective' (*jāti*). Apparently F has not realized a crucial ambivalence of this remark: The very act of clarifying that certain expressions are employed for the designation of collectives in particular contexts intimates that the pertinent expressions as types are considered as *not* always possessing such an import.

[90] The very fact that FN treats the issue in terms of the conventional query regarding the meaning of a word instead of raising a question concerning the import of the syntagma 'is *sapakṣa*' and trying to establish that this item always relates to (= is predicated of) groups or collections, signifying among others 'is (identical with the collection which is) the *sapakṣa*', consorts with a lack of proficiency in the pertinent field.

proven, i.e. the realm of all permanent objects. As far as one can see, F does not even refer to this problem to say nothing of dissolving the difficulty. If this is correct then the author of FN is not only guilty of an irresponsible simplification of the tenets of others. His faith in dubious principles of equalization makes him disregard problems of content.[91]

Originally I did not attribute major weight to the observation that F's way of rendering the term *sapakṣa* in the *pakṣasapakṣānyataratva*-argument with a definite article seems unsuitable, presuming that it was merely the outcome of a momentary inadvertence.[92] In the light

---

91 To be sure, if one took into account what is merely theoretically conceivable one could consider the possibility that the *sapakṣa*-collection of all eternal particulars is to be itself regarded as an eternal object and might therefore function as a 'positive example'. But is it plausible to assume that the proponent of the argument not only accepted this view but *presupposed* its truth in the argument itself? Should we suppose that he simply ignored the fact that teachings and schools existed which explicitly refused to acknowledge the existence of collections as genuine entities? Moreover, are we obliged to believe that the arguer, conflating groups or collections with universals or classes (in the sense of *jāti),* took for granted that *sapakṣa*-domains are eternal objects belonging themselves to them? Should one presume that the proponent of the argument completely overlooked the problems inhering in the ideas that groups or collections are elements of themselves or that there are infinite hierarchies of eternal universals among which most of them do not inhere in particular objects but in universals? As a matter of fact, all these difficulties do not arise if one drops the supposition that the import of the so-called *pakṣasapakṣānyataratva*-argument must be equivalent to: 'Sound is permanent because it is either *pakṣa* or the collection of *sapakṣa*'.

92 It might not be superfluous to point out that the constituent 'a *sapakṣa*' in the formulation 'Sound is permanent because it is either (the) *pakṣa* or a *sapakṣa'* must not be explicated in the sense of 'a *sapakṣa* in some or the other context of inference', but in the sense of 'a *sapakṣa* relative to the actual context of inference'. (This clarification was already earlier provided by me in view of the circumstance that F had mistakenly hypothesized the first explication). On the other hand it deserves to be mentioned that *if* F had employed the wording 'Sound is permanent because it is either (the) *pakṣa* or an element of the (realm of) *sapakṣa* (relative to the present context of inference)' his account would have been unobjectionable: The equivalence of the global contents of

of the remarks of FN it appears however that the original assessment was far too mild and sympathizing.[93] Anyhow, the most decisive aspect of the present issue lies in the fact that detailed analytical textual investigations are urgently needed not only because they open the possibility to weigh more meticulously the pros and cons of exegetical particulars, but also because they are apt to diminish the danger of distorting matters as a result of illegitimate imputations by paying more attention to individual features of context and co-text as well as to objective properties of content and by extending the scope of semantic investigations beyond considerations pertaining to surface level. In view of the conjecture that fundamental principles of natural languages provide for linguistic change and innovation against the background of theoretical understanding this issue possesses particular relevance.

3.

It has been contended in FN (p. 528) that the assumption that the SP predates Dignāga is 'improbable' due to the circumstance that if the SP deals with the "extrapolation principle" it ought to be later than Dignāga. If on the other hand, the SP would have been composed before Dignāga, it is highly improbable that it dealt with the

the alternative formulations is the result of a neutralization of a difference pertaining to the level of sentence constituents on the level of the sentences containing them.

93 There should be no need to discuss the 'qualities' of a principle which reads as follows: If the majority of tokens of some linguistic type T possesses the meaning M1 and not the meaning M2, then each time one encounters in a textual passage a token of T one must interpret it in the sense of M1. To be sure, matters of statistic frequency can support default rules of interpretation which could assist in speeding up one's reading in a language. But any philologist who invests only a minimum of self-reflection could easily realize that a major source of initial misunderstandings lies in implementations of unsuitable default rules and that the resultant errors are eliminated by updating information concerning a pertinent textual passage.

"extrapolation principle".[94] Moreover, the SP should be dated to the time between Dignāga and Dharmakīrti because it 'presupposes a theory of *trairūpya* as we know it from Dignāga's writings, and it also presupposes that the *trairūpya* theory had been accepted widely or even established as a norm, in order for it to be worthwhile to compose sophisms directed against it '. It looks as if F had deluded himself by deriving from the fact that the SP complies with the requirements of *trairūpya* the consequence that it was directed against this doctrine.[95] Anyhow, such a reasoning amounts to a fatal fallacy. The same would equally hold good if one based the contention that the SP was directed against *trairūpya* on the supposition that several authors — who were not historians of philosophy after all — took it in this sense.[96] For the circumstance that writers for which this doctrine had been accepted or even 'established as a norm' brought the SP in connection with it must

94 As the faultiness of this type of argument has been expounded earlier it will not be further considered here. In this connection it should be added, nevertheless, that assessments concerning dates or relative chronology in the area of ancient philosophies must pay due attention to the fact that transmission of information at those times must have been extremely slow in comparison with what would be expected nowadays.

95 To be sure, a satisfaction of all the requirements of *trairūpya* would be problematic if the existence of examples exhibiting both the absence of the quality to be proven (the *sādhya*) and the absence of the proving quality (the *hetu*) were taken as an essential ingredient of this doctrine. But first, it is not compelling to consider this element as an integral part of *trairūpya* itself. Second, *if* it were an integral element, *then* its non-satisfaction by the SP would support the hypothesis that SP was *not* 'directed' against *trairūpya*, but against a theoretical account of inference where the question of the existence of examples for the so-called *vyatireka* had not (yet) become a problem. — In this context the fact is significant that the existential commitment in question is *not* an integral part of the idea of 'inseparable connection'. One can however ascertain that the SP furnishes a possible motivation for an adoption of the postulate of the existence of 'negative examples'.

96 It should be noted in this connection that F's own contention that the SP was directed against *trairūpya* clearly disaccords with textual sources where it is supposed that the SP-argument was designed for the proof of a materialist tenet.

be expected in any case, irrespective of whether or not its original proponent intended it in this way.[97]

A major reason for questioning the alleged connection between SP and *trairūpya* lies in the existence of two textual passages which have been attributed to Vasubandhu's *Vādavidhi*. The crucial passages read as follows:

> *tādṛgavinābhāvidharmopadarśanaṃ hetuḥ*
>
> The reason is the pronouncement of a property which does not occur without a such (= which is inseparably connected with the quality to be proven).
>
> *nāntarīyakārthadarśanaṃ tadvido 'numānam*
>
> Inference is the observation of an object not occurring without [the *probandum*] for someone who knows that.

Considering those passages together one obtains the following account:

> Somebody presents a valid argument if he points out some quality [as being exhibited by some particular or plurality of particulars] if he knows that[98] [in the entire realm which remains if one leaves the

---

[97] This could be of course different, if plausible reasons existed for the hypothesis that some of the writers were personally acquainted with the original proponent of the SP (and intended to present a faithful account of something which was communicated). In the absence of such reasons, and considering the extreme unreliability of hearsay evidence, it is difficult to take seriously F's allegation (p. 527) that the supposition that the SP need not be directed against the validity of the *trairūpya* criteria 'is contradicted, explicitly or implicitly, by all the authors .... who discuss' the SP. — Note that FN does not even attempt to substantiate this contention by evidence.

[98] It deserves to be noted in passing that the SP could also be plausibly understood as being specifically 'directed' against the ingredient of knowledge pertaining to the inseparable connection between *hetu* and *sādhya*. The point is that the requirement of *knowing* the connection cannot increase the degree of cogency of an argument or even guarantee its validity because in the SP-argument the satisfaction of this postulate is most evident due to the fact that the exhibition of one of the qualities of the disjunction in the *entire* non-

items which are the objects of debate and doubt out of consideration] every item exemplifying the pertinent quality also exemplifies the quality to be proven [and that there is no exception to this rule].

Here all the essential ingredients of the *trairūpya*-doctrine are already present; the latter (viz. *trairūpya*) merely represents a further explication of the underlying idea, mainly by laying down a) that the subject of inference must in fact exhibit the proving quality or be known as exhibiting it and that mere belief that this is the case does not suffice and b) that the knowledge that the proving quality must always occur together with the quality to be proven is supported by the fact that the pertinent qualities occur together at least in some case(s). As far as the satisfaction of the criterion of the category (c)(i) is concerned it does not make a major difference whether one interprets the SP as aiming at *trairūpya* or at the underlying principle of arguing or inferring on the basis of an 'inseparable connection'.[99] It amounts moreover to a crude

---

pakṣa-realm is immediately obvious. This isrelevant not only because the falsity of the *thesis* is not obvious and because one could *not* argue that the thesis violates the postulate (which need not have been explicitly laid down at the time the SP was created!) of avoiding fallacious theses (*pakṣābhāsa).* A special strength of the SP lies also in the fact that it does not involve any explicit reference to the *concepts* of *pakṣa, sapakṣa* or *vipakṣa* and cannot be easily dismissed as relating to notions which do not stand for 'genuine qualities' in an intuitive sense. Historians of Indian philosophy seem to be too easily put out by the fact that they must think of so many 'possibilities', if they wanted to do their work properly.

[99] In view of the obvious fact that textual sources provide most immediate evidence at best for settling the latest, but not for settling the earliest possible date at which some thought has been envisaged, one must have regard to the possibility that — within reasonable limits — the origination of the concept of an inseparable connection and its exploitation for reasoning and arguing pre-dates its first manifestation in any of the existent textual sources. Considering, moreover, the intuitive simplicity and naturalness of the idea the supposition of its dating back to fairly ancient times is not eccentric. It is particularly in the context of *historical* considerations where taking such possibilities into account is important.

misrepresentation of the actual facts if one scorns the accompanying attitude as 'anti-historical'. The truth of the matter is that, in a similar way as in the context of attribution of relevance to features of co-text, an essential difference regarding significance between prior and posterior historical context is being presumed. [100] It is only the consideration of *preceding* or *contemporary* historical context that can play the role of controlling the acceptability of interpretations under the aspect of furnishing explanations for the existence of texts or of particular formulations against the background of the premise that a writer aspires to comply with the maxim of relevance in his (linguistic) behaviour.

The term 'extrapolation principle' had been employed with the purpose to allude to the underlying idea manifested both in texts like the *Vādavidhi* and, among others, in the doctrine of *trairūpya*. Hence a major reason for saying that the SP calls into question the extrapolation principle — instead of saying that it was directed against *trairūpya* — does not only lie in the purpose of bringing to light the theoretical depth of its critical potential; not less important is the circumstance that in the absence of more information one cannot simply prejudge a decision about the question as to whether or not SP

[100] In the case of preceding and subsequent co-text one can maintain that (at least by default) an interpretation should be compatible with all remarks that occur in the subsequent co-text of one and the same text and that it should preferably agree with remarks to be found in other texts of one and the same author. This represents an analogy to a methodological principle applicable in situations where, as in the case of e.g. Nāgārjuna or Śaṅkara, the authorship of certain works is uncertain: One draws a distinction between active and passive support so that any acceptable interpretation *must* possess some evidence furnished by works whose authenticity is taken for granted (in some context of investigation) whereas other works whose authenticity is (regarded as) debatable are considered under the aspect of whether or not they *would* disconfirm or shake some pertinent hypothesis *if* it were supposed that they are authentic. To that extent subsequent co-text is in principle capable of performing a criterial function. In contrast, not even this concession is permissible with respect to opinions of later interpreters (if they do not provide reliable 'insider information' provided by an original author).

originated before or after the development of *trairūpya*, in particular whether or not it was created earlier or later than the composition of Dignāga's works.

It remains incomprehensible why such caution and restraint amounts to an idle play with 'mere possibilities'.

4.

The largest part of FN is dedicated to polemics against an allegedly 'anti-historical' and futile play with possibilities contrasting it with the writer's own performances as specimens of serious scholarship, or at least insinuating such a difference. In the light of the preceding clarifications and the final remark of the last paragraph one can anticipate that the recklessness inhering in F's exposition might go beyond the presentation of fallacious arguments. This suspicion proves to be correct. It is, or should be, a fundamental principle of any science that it attempts to detach its results as far as possible from all presuppositions and premises which cannot be definitely established as true.[101] A device for enhancing the chances of truth consists in a method which can be called 'conditionalization'; this means that instead of making categorical statements resting on disputable assumptions one asserts conditional propositions where the questionable propositions occur as antecedent clauses. Here a principle is operative which underlies the rule of conditional proof in (Classical) Logic. In actual fact, that which F stigmatizes as 'play with possibilities' possesses an analogous function. In the natural sciences consideration of possibilities occurs as a vital ingredient. If, for example, certain experimental results appear to threaten some particular hypothesis or theory it is a legitimate practice to investigate all possibilities which could have caused the threatening outcome,

[101] Therefore — at least at present — interpretations of the SP must be carefully designed in such a way that its results do not vitally depend on any particular decision about its date, which means that they account for *all* (sufficiently reasonable) possibilities in this respect. Everything else amounts, from the viewpoint of the consequences, to the same as scientific fraud.

possibly causing the consideration of the possibilities that the apparently observed phenomena had been interpreted in a wrong manner, that the observations themselves were defective, that faults of measurements have occurred etc.

The reluctance to accept the method of basing decisions concerning interpretation on ways in which pertinent items were understood by later interpreters derives from the approval of the tenet that belief does not entail truth and the acknowledgment of its validity in the context of textual exegesis.[102] To be sure, the implementation of this maxim renders textual interpretation much harder and painstaking than reliance on authorities of a tradition. But in this connection something else is equally important: Purposes of theoretical analysis make it mandatory to transcend the realm of precedent intentions.

Previously two alternative versions of the SP were considered by me. They differ with respect to the extension of the domain playing the role of a *pakṣa*: Whereas in the first case the pertinent domain contains only one particular object, in the other case it is constituted by a plurality of items of the same sort. It had been assumed that not only both alternatives correspond to possible readings of the existent formulation of the SP but that a definite verdict regarding the question as to which of them represents the originally intended import is not possible under the present circumstances. Nevertheless, in some important respect the truth of those two suppositions is irrelevant. For even if it were otherwise, i.e. if at least one of the assumptions were false, the consideration of the different alternatives possesses noteworthy significance: It serves the purpose of examining whether the exhibition of relevant properties pertaining to questions of validity and

[102] It should not be concealed that the actual state of affairs is a little more intricate. One could rightly object that belief is indirectly linked up with truth due to the circumstance that the occurrence of some belief indicates (the probability of) the existence of some evidence. The decisive point is, however, that the mere existence of some evidence does not imply anything about its quality. An additional argument is required for establishing a proposition to the effect that some pertinent evidence is conclusive or highly compelling.

argumentative function of the SP rely on any particular choice among the different possibilities, and in the present case of showing that the relevant results do not depend on any particular choice among them. Under these premises, and *only* under such premises, could it be legitimate to contemplate also about the consequences of other varieties which appear linguistically less natural and presumably do not correspond to some originally intended import of the formulation, in particular a variant, propagated by F, which results by substituting the concept of numerical difference by the notion of qualitative difference.[103] Thus it emerges as a result that the SP, whatever the exact import of its original formulation might have been, is representative of an entire family of closely related variants. It is difficult to see the merits of a perspective for which such issues lie far beyond the horizon.

Primarily in the context of theoretical criticism explorations of alternatives which are not confined to previously envisaged variants can be indispensable. A most pertinent example is provided by the question of the connection between truth paradox and self-reference. The phenomenon of truth paradoxes can be used for illustrating also other aspects of the project of interpreting a theoretical tradition and is apposite to go at this point slightly deeper into this matter — touching on some issues which have not been highlighted in the preceding essay.

---

[103] A problem is that that if one would read the SP in the sense of 'The pot is unlike a pot or numerically differs from a material body endowed with consciousness, because ....' one must attribute to the expression *-sadvitīya-* two different readings at the same time, and if one would instead understand it in the sense of 'The pot is unlike a pot or unlike a material body endowed with consciousness, because ....' it becomes difficult to discern a relevant point in the SP, at least as long as one does not suppose that constructions of the form 'A is unlike a B' necessitate an existential commitment with respect to the second term of the relation. Moreover, a reference to a merely qualitative difference appears fairly improbable in view of the compositional meaning of *sadvitīya* in combination with the circumstance that other words could have been used which are far better suited for clearly signaling qualitative difference.

The conjecture that truth paradoxes are inextricably linked with self-reference can be most naturally induced by the consideration of examples involving an explicit self-reference to a linguistic item, such as

> The sentence which is uttered by me just now expresses an untruth.

A little reflection suffices however for recognizing that such explicit self-reference cannot constitute a necessary requirement in view of examples like:

> The subsequent sentence expresses a truth. The preceding sentence expresses an untruth.

or the (renowned) example of a sheet of paper where it is written on the front side:

> The sentence on the reverse side says something true.

whereas on the reverse only one sentence appears which reads:

> The sentence on the front side says something false.

etc. It turns out nevertheless that even indirect self-reference as in the above considered examples cannot play a decisive role. This is vindicated by the following case: Assume that there is a group *G* of two or three or more people such that each of them says at the same time:

> At least one member of *G* expresses an untruth just now.

To be sure, even here one could contend that some sort of self-reference is involved. However, since the concerned linguistic tokens contain only terms referring to groups of persons in the scope of quantifiers, the type of self-reference markedly differs from the specimens of self-reference in the previously considered situations. But this is not all: The predicament affecting the utterances produced by members of *G* would similarly arise if assertions with the same verbal content were made by other subjects not belonging to the pertinent group. The same holds good for statements saying for example that all the pertinent utterances made by members of *G* express a truth or for statements ascribing truth or untruth specifically to the utterances of any particular member.[104] In addition to it the so-called 'Yablo-paradox', where an actually infinite sequence of linguistic items expressing that all subsequent elements fail to express a truth is considered, poses a challenge to the contention that self-reference is a prerequisite of truth paradox.[105] No matter whether or not the tenet that paradoxes of truth depend on self-reference should be correct in the final analysis, one thing is absolutely certain: Any treatment of the problem which takes only the first explication of self-reference into account would exhibit a degree of superficiality which could never be justified, not even by the allegation that some thinker of

---

104 To give just one example. Let us suppose that *A, B* and *C* belong to the pertinent group *G* and that *D*, which does not belong to *G*, expresses a truth-denial regarding *A*. A common reasoning would run as follows: If *D* expresses a truth then *A* does not express a truth by saying that at least one member of *G* fails to express a truth. Consequently, all members of *G* must express a truth and therefore *A* expresses a truth, which contradicts the assumption that *D* expresses a truth by saying that *A* fails to express a truth. Supposing that *D* fails to express a truth it follows that *A* expresses a truth; then at least one member of *G* must fail to express a truth by saying that at least one member of *G* fails to express a truth. Accordingly, all members of *G* express a truth, because otherwise no sentence could express an untruth by saying that at least one member of *G* fails to express a truth. Hence even the assumption that *D* fails to express a truth involves a contradiction.

105 A consideration of all varieties of truth paradox is needed for critically assessing the appropriateness of calling into question a principle that can be formulated as follows:

> If some (declarative) sentence S (which does not contain indexical elements as constituents) unequivocally expresses that p, then S expresses a truth if and only if (it is the case that) p

This in turn possesses relevance for evaluating a contention saying that, in defiance of the high intuitive plausibility of this theorem, only a weaker principle which reads

> If some (declarative) sentence S (which does not contain indexical elements as constituents) unequivocally expresses that p, then S expresses a truth only if (it is the case that) p

can be accepted without reservation. — It deserves to be emphasized that thereby the validity of the principle 'It is true that p if and only if p' is *not* disputed.

the past omitted a consideration of additional possibilities. What matters in this context are not intentions connected with formulations created in the past but the question as to whether for some particular theoretical tenet an explication can be found which would render it true.[106]

It deserves to be noted in addition that, strictly speaking, the phenomenon of truth paradox encompasses at least three major subcategories. The first type, illustrated by the above considered examples, involves a direct threat of logical contradiction or inconsistency. The second variety is distinguished by the fact that inconsistency appears to be avoidable only at the cost of admitting assignments of deviant truth values on a purely arbitrary basis which provides no rationale for the deviance (except the avoidance of inconsistency itself). It can be illustrated by cases like the utterances of two colleagues saying about each other nothing else than that not a single truth is uttered about him by his counterpart or the situation in which all members of some group G say at the same time that nothing true is said by any other member of G at that time etc. A further major variety exhibits the characteristic that from assumptions, involving some sort of reference to matters of truth, consequences appear to be derivable regarding which it is (intuitively) extremely difficult to believe that they should be entailed by them. They in turn comprise different subspecies.[107] This confronts us with the tasks 1) of identifying the pertinent principles that are involved, 2) of examining which

---

106 Even under a purely historical perspective this sort of question is not necessarily irrelevant. For someone who studies the history of some philosophical or other theoretical tradition of thought it could be significant to ascertain whether certain sources reveal the occurrence of insights which were not (yet) fully explored by those who discerned them.

107 There are examples where on the basis of hypothetical assumptions, pertaining to contingent (historical) facts concerning utterances having (allegedly) been made, the existence of different assertions is derived. An illustration is provided by deriving on the basis of the assumption that some Cretan has (once) said that nothing true is ever asserted by a Cretan the conclusion that there is at least one different proposition asserted by a Cretan which is not false. Although this conclusion is presumably actually true it is

of them might be assailable and 3) of finding plausible justifications for the abandonment of those assumptions which are deemed untenable. Thus it can be quite a long way from the initial detection of a problem to its satisfactory treatment, and it should be legitimate to pose the question of how long a tradition has advanced on this path.

The problem of the relationship between self-reference and truth paradox affects all variants. If such different aspects of a theoretical issue need to be taken into consideration for obtaining a deeper understanding of the nature of problems and for assessing the potential significance of any specimen of some tradition, it cannot matter, at least in principle, whether a Western or non-Western tradition of thought is concerned. A further notable ingredient of the enterprise of relating specific facets of problems and particular ways they have been addressed by individual authors or in certain segments of a tradition of thought to a more comprehensive framework consists in the potential to enrich our own conceptual resources. In the realm of truth paradoxes there are specimens which intimate that it is a critical mark of truth paradoxes that they exhibit conclusions which involve some reference to the idea of truth. As soon as one considers those specimens in a broadercontext it emerges however that this feature is by no means essential. Only against the background of the broader perspective a suitable verdict concerning the question of whether some problem has been satisfactorily treated in thepast could be given.

In the present connection the fact is important that one can never proceed on the assumption that some tradition of thought has discovered all the variants of some phenomenon which can be detected in principle and even less can it be expected that it presents explicit accounts of relevant variances. Given, however, that an awareness of

hard to believe that the two historical facts should be related in a manner that the second follows from the first. On the other hand, one can conceive examples where even false conclusions pertaining to contingent historical matters — in fact any arbitrary true or false proposition — appear derivable from true premises which refer solely to what certain linguistic items mean or express. An illustration is given in the Appendix of this essay.

the existence of objective differences and an ascertainment of their nature can be significant even if an earlier tradition has not explicitly recognized them, a stance rejecting their identification as illegitimate merely on account of the circumstance that it does not reflect some previous awareness, and that it deals with formerly unrealized 'possibilities', is suited to hamper important progress in a field. Attention merits also the fact that it is the background of considerations like the above presented ones which permits us to assess the degree of justification and, as a matter of fact, the extremely low plausibility of a contention advocated by certain scholars to the effect that Bhartṛhari's *Sambandha-Samuddeśa* section of the *Vākyapadīya* (or *Trikāṇḍī*) should provide us with 'the key to an interesting and elegant solution' to the family of paradoxes to which the Liar Paradox belongs.[108] Achieving a better understanding of the nature of some problem or subject matter possesses even potential relevance with respect to 'traditional' varieties of interpretation aiming at the identification of intentions of foreign subjects: By recognizing in this perspective shortcomings in the treatment of some presumed topic one can realize that originally hypothesized suppositions regarding intentions and goals of language users, such as authors of a text, are questionable. This is by no means a merely theoretically conceivable possibility.[109]

The author of the PV is surely not the only philosopher who does *not* subscribe to the view that soundness of criticism deserves to be sacrificed for the sake of harmony with some original intention. Presumably the distinction which has been envisaged in PV IV, 34 and is indicated by the particle *atha* relates to the difference between a reading according to which the disjunction implicit in the SP connects whole sentences or propositions on the one hand and on the other hand a reading according to which this operator, in modern terminology, maps non-complex predicates onto complex predicates standing for

[108] Cf. Houben 1995:382, and elsewhere.

[109] Cf. Oetke 2012:45ff and 2013:9–39.

some (more general) disjunctive property. Only in the first case it can be argued that at least one of the individual propositions must be supported by a reasoning complying with the acknowledged requirements for the acceptability of individual inferences, whereas a rejection of the SP on the basis of the second alternative requires additional (and questionable) premises relating either to identity- and discriminability-conditions of universals[110] or to adequacy-conditions of using disjunctions. To be sure, other ways of understanding the nature of the envisaged alternatives have been proposed in the literature and it is neither possible nor necessary to weigh the pros and cons of the different interpretations regarding the PV in the present connection.[111] For the following contention appears to be defensible at

---

[110] The contention that universals instantiated in exactly the same particulars are indistinguishable is apt to suggest the idea that general properties can be understood as disjunctions of individual features, that for example the property of being perishable amounts to the same as the property of being a perishable sound or a perishable non-sound / a perishable pot or a perishable wall etc. The subsequent discussion in the PV intimates, however, that the author of the text did not believe that this possibility could endanger his own theoretical outlook.

[111] The mere existence of different views regarding the content of the pertinent alternative is far more significant than the doubtfulness of F's specific opinion articulated in Franco 2012:222–223, according to which the contrast should lie between an inclusive interpretation of the disjunction and some other (unspecified) reading. For this circumstance brings home to us the disadvantage of intermingling the task of interpreting some theoretical item on the one hand and that of interpreting its interpretation in a tradition on the other. The relevant danger lies in an accumulation of mistakes. The first source of possible mistakes lies in the fact that an item is assessed in the light of a context which is definitely not its own original context. The second source lies in the possibility of misinterpreting the context which presents its interpretation and criticism. The danger is virulent because not only the PV but texts representing the Indian philosophical tradition in general exhibit a considerable degree of linguistic ambiguity and vagueness. Here — as well as in many other contexts of argumentative reasoning — the previously mentioned methodological tool of assessing the relevance of a(n immediately) subsequent co-text with respect to the content of a preceding linguistic unit attains importance: The interpretation of the pertinent disjunctive alternative brings into play the

any rate: The author of the PV did not consider the two alternatives because he believed that both of them represent original intentions of the inventor of the SP but because he regarded their consideration as an indispensable requirement for the soundness of his own criticism. Instead of dismissing this attitude we ought to appreciate it as the most appropriate stance in the context of philosophical criticism. It is definitely not on *this* account that Dharmakīrti's treatment of the matter deserves to be regarded as defective; if it is nevertheless unsatisfactory, then the reason would rather lie in Dharmakīrti's omission to carefully explore whether the object of his criticism possesses the potential of throwing a critical light on the author's own philosophy.

In principle it *could* be argued that *nowadays* philosophical criticism concerning theoretical elements in the Indian philosophical tradition is improper because the teachings are outdated or too uninteresting or for other reasons, so that one might evade the obligation to consider possibilities which possess at most theoretical relevance. But the justification of this contention is disputable. One can at least definitely ascertain that FN does not even present the preliminary of an argument establishing that (at least) Indian philosophical theorems are not worth being assessed under the aspects of truth or objective significance. Should it be welcomed that because of the failure to clearly acknowledge different components of dealing with philosophical traditions the level of studies pertaining to Indian philosophies drops far behind the standards of parallel explorations pertaining to Western philosophical traditions, such as Greek philosophy or the philosophy of the Middle Ages?

It appears indeed improbable that F should be the only one who tends to belittle studies on (specimens of) foreign philosophical

---

question of whether or not the subsequent remarks referring to it can be regarded as providing a relevant and adequate answer to some proposed argument or objection. It is on this account that the above suggested understanding appears most appropriate. Anyway, the failure to employ this criterion of pragmatic and theoretical relevance for the purpose of exegetical explication in an explicit and systematic manner is a fairly pervasive phenomenon not confined to articles dealing with the SP.

traditions under other perspectives than 'history of thought' ('*Geistesgeschichte*'). Such an attitude is intimated e.g. by a number of remarks made by W. Halbfass 1997, in particular 1997:237, where it has been said, among other things, that

> the pursuit of an ideal of precision — which is (allegedly) imposed by modern logic but not by some author's, such as Dharmakīrti's, 'own orientation and its historical context' — leads to a free play with conceivable possibilities which are not concerned with the way in which some author 'really thought', but rather with the question as to how he could or rather should have thought

and that

> whoever wants to understand a thinker who orientated himself by practical and soteriological aims must try to understand his intentions, which are not purely of a theoretical and analytical character.

Since this critique has been reviewed by me earlier in more detail — Oetke 2007:571ff — only the following remarks deserve to be made in this connection:

Halbfass' criticism pertains to an undertaking that exhibits affinities with certain studies made in recent times in the field of Ancient Greek philosophy, namely of identifying premises or presuppositions implicit in particular specimens of philosophical theorizing or argumentation. Those premises are characteristically not explicitly stated in textual sources — otherwise the task of identification would be rather trivial and uninteresting. Moreover, the concerned premises and presuppositions need not be identical with thought-contents which the author of some text explicitly entertained or grasped. They could, however, be interesting on other accounts, for example because they represent propositions which, if added to the explicitly presented argumentative steps, would render the argumentation as a whole more convincing or compelling or, in the limiting case, even yield a formally valid derivation of a conclusion from assumptions. In the particular case of the analysis of Dharmakīrti's attempts of establishing universal momentariness by means of proof the project was guided by the idea that identifying 'logically relevant' premises and presuppositions of proofs aiming at vindicating theorems contradicting ordinarily accepted opinions opens a chance of detecting presuppositions underlying our common-sense views, such as the belief that there are objects (of the physical world) which persist for some time. A number of those presuppositions would presumably correspond to the negation of some of the premises which would be required for establishing the 'counter intuitive' tenets.[112] In principle, an analysis of this type can equally serve the purpose of ascertaining whether a theoretical argument in combination with certain assumptions would be suited to establish some tenet which, although differing from the one which its original proponent intended to demonstrate, is either significantly related to the envisaged one or possesses some independent (theoretical) significance. Against the background of an attempt to prove universal momentariness a theorem satisfying this criterion would be represented by the proposition that *at least some* entities possessing a momentary nature must be found in the realm of objectively existing items. This is definitely not, but merely a weaker variant of, the thesis which Dharmakīrti intended to establish, and one might presume that the (theoretical) possibility that the world is occupied by various sorts of objects, such that the (relatively) permanent ones can exhibit causal efficiency only because momentary particulars *also* exist, was not propagated in the tradition following Dharmakīrti.[113] But if it could be shown that arguments presented for

---

[112] This does, however, not hold good for all of them. Noteworthy is the circumstance that certain presuppositions of common sense seem to be equally acknowledged in the context of Dharmakīrti's argumentations for the tenet of momentariness, for example a proposition which could be characterized as the theorem of the homogeneous nature of time.

[113] This alternative would have deserved some consideration because, as it seems, the contention that existing items must actually produce (numerically

the establishment of a stronger thesis contain ingredients providing support for some weaker variant, then the mere fact that a certain tradition ignored this possibility is significant in itself.[114]

To be sure, it is in principle possible that the project of identifying presumptions of common sense remains unsuccessful, for example because it is implemented in a manner which lacks some required degree of rigor or for other reasons. It could even be argued that resorting to philosophical tradition for detecting fundamental presuppositions of common-sense is inappropriate because, maybe, a systematically orientated critical analysis of ordinary views is a more efficient means to this end. But critical considerations of this sort which would have been at least relevant for the pertinent subject matter are not raised by Halbfass. His remarks in this connection are immaterial because they hypothesize aims which were neither intended nor relevant for the concerned issue.[115] The very nature of the pursued analysis entails that concern with the way in which Dharmakīrti 'really thought' cannot be the ultimate goal. It is moreover definitely untrue that this circumstance

different) effects at any time of their existence could be equally well explained by the hypothesis of a causal collaboration between momentary and relatively persistent entities.

114 It is true that, as far as one can see, nobody up to now has thoroughly explored the question as to whether arguments for the tenet of universal momentariness presented by Dharmakīrti or others are apt to support a weaker variety of thesis than the intended one. One must also admit that it is impossible to ascertain *a priori* whether investigations of this kind would yield results which are significant and interesting. On the other hand, however, it is legitimate to assert that a discipline which rejects questions of this type as irrelevant from the outset can hardly command much respect.

115 Apart from the points a) whether aims which had been pursued really merit to be pursued as well as b) whether the pursuit of the intended aims was actually successful, also the queries c) whether efforts and expenditures for the achievement of the envisaged goals were in fact worthwhile or d) whether the same aims could have been achieved by alternative and less arduous means could have been legitimate questions. As it seems, a biased preconception of the nature of investigations on traditions of thought is responsible for the failure to pinpoint those problems which are most pertinent to some subject matter.

implies a completely free play with conceivable possibilities.[116] On the other hand, the contention that wanting to understand a particular thinker who (allegedly) orientated himself by practical and soteriological aims necessitates understanding his intentions which are not of a theoretical and analytical character lacks relevance inasmuch as it takes for granted that understanding of a person, specifically the personality of an author, *must* constitute an ultimate aim of textual analysis. Persons, however, are not the only admissible objects of understanding: Apart from linguistic items like words or sentences, argumentations, teachings and theories are equally legitimate objects. By analysing them in particular one does not *eo ipso* disclaim the possibility of 'practical' or even 'soteriological' intentions. In the present context the allegation of the existence of intentions of the latter kind could obtain relevance at most on the understanding that persons are concerned who did not pursue theoretical aims at all. Hence it would have been incumbent on the author of the above quoted remarks to prove such a contention in the first instance.[117] As might be expected, such a proof is nowhere presented.

It could be deemed appropriate to abstain from further critical investigations about FN because nothing else could discredit the article more than the crude and unsophisticated manner in which it deals with the issue of 'possibilities'.

---

[116] A most important restriction is imposed by the requirement that the additional hypotheses should license a pertinent conclusion only in combination with the arguments which are explicitly advanced in a textual source. After all, every argumentation could be transformed into a valid derivation of a conclusion from assumptions in a trivial manner simply by adding the conclusion itself to the set of premises. A violation of the maxim to consider only additional hypotheses that are significant in the explicated sense would be certainly detrimental to the undertaken project of analysis. By not even perceiving this facet of the matter Halbfass misses from the outset a further possibility to embark on some potentially relevant critical investigation.

[117] It would be a serious mistake to raise the objection that theoretical practice is an exclusively Western phenomenon. In the present connection one needs to sharply differentiate between pursuit of theoretical aims and pursuit of theoretical aims for the sake of theory.

However, at least the following two points deserve to be brought up too. They equally possess implications that go beyond the particular topic of the SP.

5.

FN contends (p. 527) that one must address the question whether the Lokāyata tradition, with which the SP is affiliated, was concerned with the "extrapolation principle". Why should we assume that the Lokāyata tradition is 'affiliated' with the SP? Perhaps because the conclusion of the SP represents a Lokāyata tenet? That would amount to a further specimen of fallacy.

Arguing against a fundamentalist Christian I could be easily motivated to present an argument showing that *if* one accepted his ways of reasoning then one could equally establish tenets propagated by the Salafists. Do I thereby become a Salafist? At any rate, lines of reasoning uncritically deriving an affiliation of an (original) proponent of some argument from the character of the conclusion should be preferably avoided in any discipline which desires to be taken seriously. Reliance on explicit attributions on the part of a posterior tradition — there are in fact (much) later sources (e.g. the *Pramāṇavārttikavṛtti*) attributing the SP to the 'Cārvākas' — does by itself not improve the situation to a relevant degree. For the crucial question is: What were the (original) reasons for the pertinent ascriptions? — By not taking for granted that the SP was (originally) designed by a proponent of Cārvāka I am disposed to deviate from opinions of various other writers who wrote on the topic, even if this should relativize my previous contentions concerning the potential significance of 'marginalized' traditions, such as that of the 'materialists'.

Accordingly one cannot simply take for granted that the doctrinal affiliation of the inventor of the SP was different from that of e.g. the originator of the *pakṣasapakṣānyataratva*-argument. Perhaps both items go even back to one and the same person, someone who intended to show, that in the framework of a *Vādavidhi*-type theory tenets held by different schools are equally derivable, and illustrated this fact by various examples. If one accepted the line of argument of FN (see in particular the section beginning with: 'Given that the work where the sp was expounded for the first time ....', p. 526) it should be possible to validly object: 'But there is no textual evidence for this assumption'. Here we are again confronted with the threat of a criticism which would exhibit a lack of elementary scientific reflection. Whenever one deals with a supposition for which textual evidence of some particular sort cannot be found, one is obliged to address the question: 'How probable is it that if the supposition *were* true then textual evidence of the pertinent kind *would* exist?' If the probability is high then absence could certainly yield a sound objection. But if this is not the case one cannot legitimately derive that the supposition must be false or could be completely ignored. The only sober consequence to be drawn is to clearly acknowledge that, at least for the time being, the matter must be treated as undecided and to take care that all future conclusions do not depend on either a positive or a negative verdict.

6.

Cases might exist where *both* parties had not reached a proper understanding of each other. For example, FN contends (p. 530) that the *sādhya* in the SP amounts to 'either not being a pot or not being a conscious body', which the author represents by '$(\neg P) \vee (\neg Q)$', where 'P' should stand for something's being a pot and 'Q' for something's being a conscious body. Accordingly the *vyatireka* should read: 'whatever is a pot and a conscious body is a lotus'. This in its turn should, according to FN, amount to 'whatever is a conscious body is a lotus', if one wants to exclude the *pakṣa* from the *vyāpti*. It is the last step to which I cannot attribute the slightest plausibility. At least I can say that when I on my part speak of an exclusion of the *pakṣa* in the *vyatireka* or *vyāpti*, or whatever else, I never contend that this affects in any way the identity of the qualities to be proven (*sādhya*) and the qualities which function as the reason (*hetu*) but only the question of the domain where exemplification or non-exemplification of the pertinent qualities matter for validity. My own account of the *vyatireka* would be entirely different and could be, in a fully explicit form, paraphrased by: '(In the domain outside the *pakṣa* it holds true that:) Everything which neither possesses a (second = different) counterpart in the form of a man characterizable as a body where consciousness is manifested nor a (second = different) counterpart in the form of the/a pot which functions as *pakṣa* is (not) a (non-)lotus'. The truth of this proposition is guaranteed by the impossibility of something's not being *pakṣa* and at the same time not differing from it, as long as one does not hypothesize some existential commitment to the effect that there are (actual) things exhibiting absence of *sādhya* and *hetu*. (Here the formulation 'everything which .... is ....' abbreviates the phrase 'everything is such that, if it .... , then ....' — where 'if .... then ...' possesses the import of a material conditional. This reading is appropriate because the *vyatireka* ought to be equivalent to the *anvaya*).

What matters for the present context of argumentation can only be the import which I assigned to the notion of an exclusion of the *pakṣa* and not anything which F might associate with that idea because the pertinent issue must pertain to an allegation on the part of F concerning something stated by me. Moreover, as far as the purely systematic aspect of the topic is concerned, it can be clearly ascertained that the SP contains the potential for posing a valid problem for any theoretical framework containing an exclusion of the *pakṣa* in the above portrayed sense as an ingredient. Apart from this it is however, pace F and FN, also maintained by me that a framework of this sort possesses historical significance inasmuch as its existence can have provided a motivation for propagating the SP. — It should be noted in passing that textual or other historical support for F's alternative conception of exclusion of a *pakṣa* has not (yet) been presented. — On the one hand the fact that F has patently distorted the import intended by me dissolves possible apprehensions to the effect that absence of major dissent might annihilate the relevance of the previously given remarks and clarifications concerning the SP. After all the position originally advocated by me, according to which the SP was (at least also) meant as a criticism of particular accounts of inferential reasoning and was not, as suggested by a number of earlier authors, exclusively designed for proving a materialistic tenet by resorting to fallacious and 'sophistic' arguments, essentially amounts to a corroboration of a view advanced by F himself. On the other hand, however, the circumstance that a subsequent debate, instead of unveiling some basis of commonly shared principles, brings only divergences and (mutual?) misinterpretations to light, intimates that the area of studies on Indian philosophies is affected by a deeper subjacent defect.

III

FN itself diminishes the credibility of the tenet that reliance on what interpreters believe and say furnishes a useful basis for making decisions in matters of interpretation by showing that at present criticism without proper understanding in fact occurs.[118] There is no reason to suppose that this phenomenon is confined to the milieu of present Western scholars. F's complaints to the effect that he himself has been misunderstood cannot eliminate the self-defeating ingredient of his paper. On the contrary, even if his allegations should be really founded and not merely pleaded, it would only all the more follow that interpreting something in the light of its reception by others is a dubious enterprise.[119] F has surely a right to demand that he should be interpreted in a fair manner. But the same right which he claims for himself should also be conceded to others, including those who wrote texts in the remote past.

---

[118] An essential source of F's deficiency of understanding lies also in his failure to recognize the existence of different alternative *questions*: Without disputing the importance of identifications of actual intentions in general it can be asserted that in cases where reliable information about an original context is deficient the query of what was *really* intended by someone tends to be less fruitful than the question as to what somebody could have *reasonably* intended by something.

[119] It should go without saying that this does in no way affect the question of the legitimateness of investigating a history of reception for its own sake, not only in the form of its description, but particularly in the form of its critical evaluation.

Appendix

Let (S) be a sentence(-token) which reads:

> That which (S*) linguistically expresses is true.

and (S*) a sentence(-token) which reads:

> If that which (S) linguistically expresses is true then Napoleon Bonaparte was born in Athens.

Let 'N' be an abbreviation for 'Napoleon Bonaparte was born in Athens'.

Now let us further suppose that both (S) and (S*) comply with a principle (P) which reads:

> For any declarative sentence s: If s linguistically expresses that p, then that which s thereby expresses is true if and only if p.

This would license the following two propositions:

> If (S) linguistically expresses that that which (S*) linguistically expresses is true, then that which (S) thereby expresses is true, if and only if, that which (S*) linguistically expresses is true.

> If (S*) linguistically expresses that if that which (S) linguistically expresses is true then N, then that which (S*) thereby expresses is true, if and only if, if that which (S) linguistically expresses is true then N.[120]

---

[120] Although formulations, such as:

> If (S) (linguistically) expresses that (S*) is true, then (S) is true, if and only if, (S*) is true.

> If (S*) (linguistically) expresses that if (S) is true then N, then (S*) is true, if and only if, if (S) is true then N

or

> If (S) means that (S*) is true, then (S) is true, if and only if, (S*) is true.

Let us hereafter employ ‘express’ instead of ‘linguistically express’, such that the shorter expression possesses the same import as its longer counterpart. Moreover, let us employ ‘T x’ as a shorthand for ‘that which x (linguistically) expresses is true’, ‘&’ in the sense of ‘and’, ‘$\leftrightarrow$’ in the sense of ‘if and only if’ and ‘$\rightarrow$’ in the sense of ‘if .... then ....’, ‘v’ in the sense of (inclusive) ‘or’ and ‘$\neg$’ in the sense of ‘It is not the case that’. Now we can present the following sequence of derivational steps:

1	(1)	(S) expresses that $T(S^*) \rightarrow [T(S) \leftrightarrow T(S^*)]$	A(ssumption)
2	(2)	(S^*) expresses that $[T(S) \rightarrow N] \rightarrow [T(S^*) \leftrightarrow [T(S) \rightarrow N]]$	A
3	(3)	(S) expresses that $T(S^*)$	A
4	(4)	(S^*) expresses that $[T(S) \rightarrow N]$	A
1,3	(5)	$T(S) \leftrightarrow T(S^*)$	(From) 1,3 (by) Modus Ponendo Ponens
2,4	(6)	$T(S^*) \leftrightarrow [T(S) \rightarrow N]$	2,4 Modus Ponendo Ponens
7	(7)	$T(S)$	A
1,3,7	(8)	$T(S^*)$	5,7 Modus Ponendo Ponens
1,2,3,4,7	(9)	$T(S) \rightarrow N$	6,8 Modus Ponendo Ponens
1,2,3,4,7	(10)	N	7,9 Modus Ponendo Ponens
1,2,3,4	(11)	$T(S) \rightarrow N$	7,10 Conditional Proof
1,2,3,4	(12)	$T(S^*)$	6,11 Modus Ponendo Ponens
1,2,3,4	(13)	$T(S)$	5,12 Modus Ponendo Ponens
1,2,3,4	(14)	N	11,13 Modus Ponendo Ponens

(The leftmost numbers refer to the assumptions on which the respective lines depend; assumptions are treated as depending on themselves. It ought to be kept in mind that the above portrayal is a condensed representation of a derivation where instead of expressions of the form

---

> If (S^*) means that if (S) is true then N, then (S^*) is true, if and only if, if (S) is true then N

would be more convenient, they exhibit a deficit of explicitness which entails relevant shortcomings in certain connections. Nevertheless, in the present context it would not cause damage if the original formulations were taken in the sense of one or another of the simplified variants.

'A ↔ B' expressions of the form '(A → B) & (B → A)' occur and where accordingly the rule of '&-Elimination' comes into play too).

The only substantial premises on which the conclusion that Napoleon Bonaparte was born in Athens depends relate to what certain linguistic units mean or express. It is easy to see that 'N' could symbolize in principle any proposition whatsoever. Accordingly, any arbitrary true or untrue proposition can be established on the basis of appropriate assumptions relating merely to what linguistic items mean or (linguistically) express. The sequence of derivational steps could be extended by adding a deduction leading from the assumption of the negation of 'N', or any proposition represented by this symbol, to the conclusion that at least one of the assumptions pertaining to the meaning or verbal content of linguistic expressions must be untrue. It appears, however, legitimate to refrain from a detailed exposition of this aspect here.

To be sure, a crucial role for the whole derivation is played by the above specified principle (P). If this principle were given up, or more specifically, excluded from truth value attributions to other truth value attributions the basis for deriving the paradox would lapse.

A similar role is played by a postulate connecting meaning with asserted content in a manner according to which the asserted content exactly mirrors the linguistic meaning (or verbal content) of a declarative sentence not containing any indexical elements. If it cannot be tacitly supposed that from the supposition that a Cretan utters words linguistically expressing that no truth has ever been uttered by a Cretan it follows that he has asserted precisely that which his words mean, the derivation of paradoxes which seem to be licensed otherwise loses its conclusiveness. This implies that there is a concept of assertion which needs to be detached from that of a speaker's or writer's intention.[121]

Intuitively, a principle which reads:

[121] There are things which a speaker cannot assert even if he intended to assert them because by trying to assert them he is (possibly without knowing it) bound to assert something in addition.

> For any speaker U and any sentence s: If U asserts or says by (using) s that p, then that which s thereby asserts or says is true if and only if p.

appears incontrovertible and one could indeed acknowledge its legitimacy. The crucial point is, however, that *if* one admits its validity, one is obliged to critically reflect on the question of what (type of content) ought to be regarded as that which a speaker (or writer) by assertively uttering a linguistic unit thereby asserts or says.

A more detailed exposition of the topic is presented in the first essay.

Retrospection

I

The article with the title 'Final Notes on the *Sadvitīyaprayoga'* (= FN) is the fifth member of a series of interrelated papers which deal with a particular piece of reasoning whose inventor(s) and advocates are usually believed to be affiliated to the tradition of Indian 'materialism' and which is associated with the denomination *Sadvitīyaprayoga* (= SP). The pertinent list consists of the following papers:

(A) A Note on the Sadvitīyaprayoga. Journal of Indian Philosophy, 40, 2012, pp. 219–224 [F]

(B) A Brief Appraisal of the *Sadvitīyaprayoga. Journal of Indian Philosophy*, 41, 2013, pp. 43–55 [O]

(C) Further notes on the *Sadvitīyaprayoga. Journal of Indian Philosophy*, 41, 2013, pp. 665–670 [F]

(D) Additional Notes on the *Sadvitīyaprayoga. Journal of Indian Philosophy*, 44, 2016, pp. 507–523 [O]

(E) Final Notes on the *Sadvitīyaprayoga. Journal of Indian Philosophy*, 44, 2016, pp. 525–535 [F]

— The symbols '[F]' and '[O]' indicate articles written by E. Franco and C. Oetke respectively.

The significance of (A) derives in the first place from the fact that it advocates the thesis that in the SP the purpose of the original proponent of this inference, who is supposed to be a Cārvāka, 'was probably not primarily to establish that a person is nothing but a body in which consciousness is manifested .... but to show a serious deficiency in the structure of inference that allows any odd thesis to be established, and consequently that inference should not be considered a reliable means of knowledge, especially not for establishing metaphysical entities such as God and Soul' (p. 223). This implies an important deviation from views intimated by earlier writers on the topic of the SP where it was supposed that the inference should demonstrate the truth of a tenet held by the 'materialists'. The very idea that the overriding function of the SP is of a critical nature deserves serious consideration and there are good reasons to believe that it is also true. Accordingly the objective of (B) was not to cast doubts on this conjecture, but on the contrary to enhance its plausibility by segregating the essence of the pertinent tenet from ingredients which were deemed less essential and could diminish its credibility, especially in view of the circumstance that it contradicts opinions of authors representing the tradition of the reception of the SP, such as Dharmakīrti and others. For achieving this goal (B) has focused on objective properties of the SP inasmuch as they can be safely inferred from the mere wording of that specimen of reasoning. In this manner one is enabled to recognize

(a) that the critical potential inhering in the SP reaches deeper than making apparent 'the bankruptcy of the *trairūpya* doctrine', as suggested in (A), and

(b) that its potential relevance extends even beyond any account of inferential reasoning which could be supposed to have existed prior to the time of its original creation, whereas

(c) it is, from an objective viewpoint, inept to license the bold conclusion that inference cannot be considered a reliable means of knowledge.

II

This way of considering the matter possesses both historical and a-historical strands which call for an exact identification because their confusion proves to be fatal:

1.

The investigation employs a procedure of content-determination whose essential trait could be characterized as 'contextual suspension' or 'contextual bracketing (ἐποχή)' on account of the fact that it exclusively exploits linguistic (lexical, syntactic and compositional) data, leaving considerations of possible contextual features out of consideration. There are countless linguistic items, particularly declarative sentences lacking indexical constituents, for which this method of content-identification is legitimate and widely practiced in ordinary life. For sentence(-token)s, such as

> There is exactly one prime number which is greater than 5 and smaller than 11.
>
> Water can evaporate if it is heated.

etc. it is obviously possible to determine a kind of content relevant for questions of truth responsible for logical properties, such as entailment, without embarking on prior investigations concerning place, time of utterance or biographical details of the utterer. Nothing but recognition of this fairly trivial fact is needed for comprehending with respect to the SP the nature of the pertinent content-determination as well as the basis of its legitimacy. There is no need to deny that the SP brings in its wake some intricacies not involved in the above cited example-sentences, such as the vagueness regarding the definiteness of nouns and noun-phrases. The decisive point is, however, that once some wording is accepted,[122] the questions can be suitably handled without definitely settling queries concerning original context. For abstaining from prejudging questions of context is certainly not

---

[122] In the pertinent context of discussion the formulation

> *abhivyaktacaitanyaśarīralakṣaṇapuruṣaghaṭānyatarasadvitīyo ghaṭaḥ, anutpalatvāt,* ***kuḍyavat***

is taken as basis, assuming that variants, such as *-ghaṭayor anyatareṇa sadvitīyo* (instead of *-ghaṭānyatarasadvitīyo*), which might possess significance in the context of textual criticism, may be disregarded in view of the relevant purposes of investigation tantamount to disregarding semantic indeterminacies: Those are and *need* to be accounted for by acknowledging, as in linguistics, alternative possible readings and interpretations. Although actual mental processes of disambiguation in ordinary linguistic interactions might often follow other patterns, it is a viable methodological device — which might even be implemented in computer-programs — to subdivide processes of interpretation into a) a component of linguistic disambiguation yielding (linguistically) possible readings as outputs and b) a component of determination where in the light of contextual information, if available, decisions between the alternative possibilities are achieved. Against the possible reproach that an account bringing only the first component into play is a-historical inasmuch as it disregards the fact that (presumably) there *was* a historical context in which the SP originally occurred, a clear and blunt answer is appropriate: There is no other legitimate alternative than presenting possibilities *as* possibilities.

Notwithstanding the a-historical aspect resulting from suspending certain judgments about historical context and the a-temporal nature exhibited by considered logical properties of identified contents, the pertinent contemplations concerning the SP possess historically relevant implications: The fact, that the objective critical potential of the SP reaches deeper than questioning the *trairūpya*-doctrine in combination with the fact that it cannot validly license the 'bold contention' that no sort of inference can function as a source of (fairly reliable) knowledge, implies that somebody who employs the SP for establishing those claims would act less reasonably than somebody who uses this device for demonstrating instead that some particular account of inference cannot be adequate and fails to perform the function which it should perform. Given a) that one can think of accounts of inference which are, as a matter of fact, affected by the criticism inhering in the SP and which need not refer to *trairūpya* and given in addition b) that it is quite probable that such accounts actually existed, it is legitimate to presume that the SP was invented for casting doubts on the accounts concerned. The decisive point does not rely on a requirement to the effect that thereby the hypothesis envisaged in (A) is definitely refuted. What matters most is rather the illumination of the argumentative situation: It has become manifest that a defender of the position advanced in (A) would need to provide additional arguments for vindicating the contention that either the inventor or some advocates of the SP linked it up with a goal which is theoretically less appropriate than alternative objectives. On the other hand, any demonstration to the effect that the SP can *also* be associated with alternative objects of criticism, which are at least not less plausible, provides support for the primary tenet according to which the reasoning embodied in the SP possessed a critical function.

A dissociation of the SP from the problem of 'negative examples', which in (A) (p. 222) had been mentioned in connection with it, leads to similar results. As a matter of fact, the theoretical basis of the requirement of 'negative examples' illustrating absence of the *probandum* in combination with absence of *probans* is pretty questionable. Whoever sees a problem due to the absence of (actually existing) negative examples is bound to see a problem in the legitimateness of any inferences establishing the instantiation of a universally instantiated property in some particular case or domain. Apart from a lack of intuitive plausibility for any sweeping dismissal of such inferences it matters also that in both the Buddhist and the non-Buddhist traditions views are attested which definitely imply their acceptability. Consequently the behaviour of an advocate of the SP acknowledging the postulate of negative examples would be decisively less reasonable than the behaviour of somebody who does not recognize it as valid. In this connection it does not even matter whether the SP was employed for purposes of criticism or for the purpose of proving a materialistic tenet. Those facts taken together vindicate the hypothesis that the SP has at some time performed a critical function directed against some theoretical account of inference which did not (yet) contain the doctrine of *trairūpya* and which did not (yet) consider the absence of (actually existing) negative examples as a relevant problem has good chances of being true.

2.

The link between a-historical considerations and consequences pertaining to matters of history exists because, by identifying contents corresponding to linguistically possible readings under 'contextual suspension' and assessing reasonability-relations between acts of expressing the pertinent contents and possible functions of expressing them, one obtains a basis for probability-evaluations of possible historical courses. In situations where reliable information about details of context is missing this method provides a most important tool for purposes of exegesis. In addition to this, deliberations about reasonability-connections of the described kind constitute a suitable tool for comparing probabilities with respect to alternative contents whenever they are equally licensed by linguistic criteria, and they can be used for controlling the legitimacy of assigning preferences between alternatives. On the other hand, the view that a-historical considerations pertaining to properties of and relations between contents are only justified in so far as they possess more or less direct consequences for matters of history is highly problematic. In genuinely theoretical disciplines surprising discoveries of consequences entailed by axioms, theorems or tenets that have never been recognized before tend to possess highest significance. At present the question to which extent investigations of philosophical traditions might lead to such discoveries can be left open.

3.

One could think that assessments of historical courses in accordance with their implications concerning reasonability of personal behaviour are appropriate at best as a stopgap compensating for lack of pertinent empirical knowledge. However, a stance on this issue is tied up with one's conceptions about history of thought or '*Geistesgeschichte*'. On the one hand one might see the goal of investigating '*Geistesgeschichte*' in identifying actual historical courses and finding explanations for individual historical events. This contrasts with a conception according to which actual occurrences are considered against the background of unrealized alternatives and evaluated under aspects such as relative adequacy of means to specific goals or the relative reasonability of pursuing particular aims or of adopting certain kinds of behaviour etc. One might use the terms 'descriptive history of ideas' — '*deskriptive Geistesgeschichte*' — and 'critical history of ideas' — '*kritische Geistesgeschichte*' — for signalling the pertinent difference of conception.

The possible objection that, by approving the latter variety of '*Geistesgeschichte*', one permits subjective ingredients to be brought into play is valid at best to a limited extent: It might be indeed true that, if matters of everyday practice or areas which constitute the subject matter of political and social sciences are at stake, it can be pretty difficult to assess alternative possibilities as more or less adequate or reasonable only on the basis of objectively sound considerations. But there are also areas where things are different. For example the question whether some linguistic theory provides a materially adequate account of certain kinds of data, e.g. in the fields of morphology or syntax, and whether or not there could be alternative theories equally adequately accounting for the pertinent data in a manner which employs a smaller set of rules, should be (in many cases at least) decidable without referring to subjective prejudice. It is a privilege of theoretical 'hard' sciences, to which parts of linguistics and philosophy belong, that they provide numerous occasions for evaluating alternatives under aspects, such as adequacy and reasonability, without having to rely on subjective bias or prejudgments.

In answer to the demurral that the mere viability of a sort of investigation does not vindicate their relevance and utility the following deserves to be said:

1. If the question of relevance and utility poses a problem for 'critical *Geistesgeschichte*' it is only fair to confront 'descriptive *Geistesgeschichte*' with the same problem. The mere consideration that, as far as the exploration of Indian philosophies is concerned, the presently prevalent practice tallies more with the descriptive than the critical variety can hardly yield an objectively valid argument

— even if it could serve as a means of promoting personal interests or offer subjective relief for those who cannot do anything else.

2. In view of the circumstance that critical *Geistesgeschichte* contains the descriptive variant as an integral part it is unlikely that the variety which is orientated by a relatively narrower perspective possesses more significance.
3. Critical *Geistesgeschichte* encompasses as a possible task the detection of absences which (usually) lie beyond the scope of descriptive accounts. There is no compelling reason to believe that discoveries to the effect that certain kinds of phenomena do *not* occur in some area must be less significant than observations of existing items.
4. Contrasting actual with possible alternative happenings or courses of events provides a means of discerning characteristic features in a conceptually richer and more differentiated descriptive framework.
5. Evaluating actual occurrences in the light of alternative possibilities is apt to shed light on the contextual background in which they are embedded. This holds good for evaluations under the aspect of adequateness and reasonability in particular. For example, the circumstance that Dharmakīrti did not exploit specific formal properties of the SP for scrutinizing his own theory of *svabhāvapratibandha* and in particular his views on causality, justifies the verdict that under a perspective of pure theoretical interest his attitude was not completely adequate. Given that recognition of problems represents a dominant goal in theoretical philosophy and that negligence of problems constitutes a defect, it would be reasonable to pose the question whether the discovery that even indisputable knowledge of an invariable regularity in a domain cannot guarantee its inviolability in another domain disconfirms the view that the ascertainment of the causal character of some regularity offers a secure protection against the analogous danger that genuine causal laws operative in a domain under

> specific framework-conditions — which are causal laws inasmuch as they licence subjunctive conditional propositions — fail to be operative in other domains. The circumstance that (as far as one can see) the SP did not produce such an effect in the tradition of Buddhist philosophy intimates that the philosophical environment was not particularly conducive to such critical self-reflection. This can be partly explained by the absence of a theoretical framework helping to identify formal properties of propositions, which, the other way around, highlights the significance of logical theories. On the other hand, it can be vindicated that recognition of the probabilistic nature of inferences from effects to causes as well as the idea of a restricted validity of causal laws were apt to unsettle central ingredients of Buddhist and non-Buddhist ideologies prevailing at the time, in particular the conception of means of salvation. The omission of raising radical doubts harmonizes with a conservative attitude, which *we* should preferably avoid if we are interested in theoretical and scientific progress.

At this place it can be said in passing that considerations of objective adequacy and reasonability are not merely capable of providing a basis for assigning evaluations to abstract possibilities licensed by purely linguistic rules or conventions and of controlling the legitimacy of choices among alternative readings. There are instances where a diagnosis of lack of reasonability given some envisaged interpretation(s) provides a suitable motivation for searching for novel interpretations which are free from similar defects. As mentioned before, a section of the so-called *Sambandha-Samuddeśa* contained in Bhartṛhari's *Vākyapadīya* (*Trikāṇḍī*) had been interpreted in a manner which entails that its author must have treated a significant philosophical problem in a fairly inadequate manner. By taking this deficiency as a reason for seeking after some alternative exegesis one is able to establish that a reading exists which allows one to regard the entire section as furnishing a consistent and plausible argumentation for a reasonable tenet.[123] Under such premises it should be unjustified to discard the suggestion on no other account than its deviance from traditional interpretations represented by commentaries.

It is easy to anticipate the objection that something which appears to us (most) reasonable need not appear to others (most) reasonable and that evaluations under the aspect of reasonability can lead to distortions due to 'impositions' of rationality-concepts cherished by an interpreter to subjects whose works and creations are to be interpreted. There should be no need to dispute this truism. A fairly judicious reader must have recognized that the preceding remarks do not amount to the recommendation to adopt only interpretations which make appear foreign subjects most reasonable according to our standards. Nevertheless, a presumption to the effect that something which we regard as reasonable can also be deemed reasonable by others is certainly not illogical, and the attitude to hypothesize, without special evidence, standards and rankings of reasonability which run contrary to our standards and rankings is quite perverse. Accordingly, as long as specific arguments are not presented, one should never accept a contention to the effect that the SP should be *preferably* understood as an attempt to refute the validity of *any* kind of inferential reasoning by demonstrating that a doctrine of *trairūpya* where the postulate of 'negative examples' occurs as an integral part 'goes bankrupt', an attempt which quite obviously confronts the proponent with the problem of avoiding the threat of self-contradiction — which can be eliminated only by providing a restrictive delimitation of the term 'inference'. Also demurrals resorting to allegations concerning putative differences between Western and non-Western conceptions of rationality — or even the (bizarre) contention that rationality is a specific Western phenomenon — could not essentially alter the situation. Supposing that Western and non-Western standards of rationality are absolutely 'incommensurable' causes the problem of showing that acquisition of reliable knowledge about non-Western traditions of

---

123 A presentation of this reading has been given in Oetke 2016.

thought is possible at all. Otherwise it could be supposed that standards of rationality are not fundamentally different, that there are areas of overlap or that even a commonly shared core exists which only needs to be detected. In that case embarking on projects of 'critical *Geistesgeschichte*' could perform the significant function of purifying our present conceptions of rationality and reasonability from parochial ingredients.

III

Among other points of dispute which *could* be regarded as dispensable in view of the circumstance that they do not concern central issues of the original topic there are some which still deserve to be considered because they possess interest in other regards.

The main objective of the present section is to expose the fallacious character of deriving from the fact that a term does not exhibit linguistic ambiguity the conclusion that it must represent precisely one concept.

Vehement objections are raised both in (C) and (E) against the contention formulated in (B), p. 47, to the effect that 'raising the question of whether or not the advocates of the *sadvitīyaprayoga* attempted to establish a concomitance or *vyāpti* .... can be misleading'. The contention was directed against remarks in (A), p. 221, such as: 'the unfounded assumption in the above-mentioned studies is that the Cārvāka attempts to establish a vyāpti', '[i]n fact, there is no concomitance between the reason and the property to be proved'.[124] In (C), p. 666, it is said, among other things:

[124] The continuation, which reads:

> This is clear in the formulation of the vyatireka: Wherever there is no sadvitīyatva with a pot or a person (e.g., in ākāśa), there is no anutpalatva. But that is not true because ākāśa is not a lotus. If one objects, however, that the relationship between ākāśa, assumed here to be an unreal entity, and the absence of the property "not being a lotus" is open to various interpretations and is problematic, one can observe that the vyāpti is doubtful in the anvaya too,

> precisely because the pot is not accompanied by a pot and it is doubtful whether it is accompanied by a person as defined above.

confronts a careful reader with several problems:

1) Why did the author say that the composite phrase 'Wherever there is no *sadvitīyatva* with a pot or a person (e.g., in *ākāśa*), there is no *anutpalatva'*, i.e. 'Anything which is neither different from the/a pot nor a person (conceived as a conscious body), is not a non-lotus' is not true *because* the ether (*ākāśa*) is not a lotus? One should think that, *if* the ether were taken as some existing entity, then, due to the fact that the ether would be something different from a pot it could not hold true of it that it *neither* differs from the/a pot *nor* from a person (or anything else), so that this example cannot present a counter-instance to the complex proposition. The only item which is apt to render the *vyatireka*-phrase false, provided that persons conceived as conscious bodies do not exist, would be a pot which functions as a subject of inference (*pakṣa*), given that it is not a lotus, i.e. it is not true of it that it is not a non-lotus.

2) If ether (*ākāśa*) were not acknowledged as a really existing item it could not function as an instance contradicting the content of the *vyatireka*-proposition. One might maintain that, since it cannot be truly said of ether as a non-existing item that it is either different from a pot or a person, one might suppose that ether is neither different from a pot nor a person. But what could under those circumstances justify the assumption that it is not true that there is no *anutpalatva* in ether, i.e. that, as a matter of fact, some property or universal of being not a lotus is exemplified by or inheres in ether? Unfortunately, the author of the above quoted passage does not tell us, which possible 'interpretation' of 'absence of the property "not being a lotus" ' he has in mind. The best guess seems to be that, given that (the existence of) absences (in the sense of the technical term *abhāva*) presuppose some real substratum where they are instantiated or occur, it cannot be supposed that ether might function as a substratum for the absence of the property of not being a lotus, or any other absence, and that accordingly ether might on the one hand satisfy the requirement implicit in the antecedent of the *vyatireka*, viz. that it is not different either from a pot or a person, whereas, on the other hand, it does not satisfy the requirement of being a substratum of absence of the property 'not being a lotus'. But in this case the (alleged) non-compliance with the *vyatireka* is a result of its *formulation* in terms of absences. Hence it cannot be maintained that non-compliance with the *vyatireka* discredits the *anvaya* or the *vyāpti* in the *anvaya*, because a statement saying that any item which is a non-lotus is either different from the/a pot or a person as a conscious body does not necessitate that its corresponding contraposition is conceived in terms of absences. To suppose, however, that the advocates of

> I am not aware, however, of a discussion whether a pakṣa should be excluded from a vyāpti (or avinābhāva or similar terms for invariable concomitance).[125]

In (E), p. 529, it is again emphasized that 'not a single text passage' has been produced 'as evidence for such a discussion'.

First of all, it should be a triviality that non-existence of a discussion about the usage of a certain term does not imply anything about the actual way of employing it. That speakers of a language use expressions without discussing the way they use them corresponds to a most common practice. As the contention that the *probans* and the *probandum* in the SP are connected in a manner which can be characterized by expressions, such as '(invariable) concomitance' or 'pervasion', does clearly not involve a claim to the effect that there were discussions about words designating the pertinent connection, it remains unclear what the author of (C) and of (E) wants to prove by his remarks. Against the background of the avowal on the part of the writer of (C), p. 666, that he 'had in mind ... a *vyāpti* .... as in Dharmakīrti's works' it appears most natural to extract from the statements an argument to the effect that

---

the SP subscribed to such a view, could amount to a serious 'anachronism'. Hence the only basis for casting doubts on the '*vyāpti* in the *anvaya*' lies in the supposition that a pervasion = *vyāpti* between the properties functioning as *probans* and *probandum* must hold good in an unrestricted domain of which the substratum of inference (*pakṣa*) is a member.

125 The continuation reads:

> But independently of that, it seems unlikely that the postulate of an invariable concomitance of the kind favoured by Oetke is satisfied by the sadvitīyaprayoga. Consider the vyatireka (while putting all pots aside): Whatever is not different from a person (in the materialistic sense) is not a non-lotus (i.e., is a lotus). But a person, whether it exists or not, is not a lotus.

The reason for characterizing this statement as 'surprising' and 'puzzling' in (D), p. 511, was that the *vyatireka* presented there in (C) neither reflects a concomitance 'favored' by me nor anything which should be expected, given the fact that the corresponding *anvaya* must exhibit a disjunctive component since the *probandum* of the SP is disjunctive.

a) Dharmakīrti (and some others) employed *vyāpti* in a sense which prohibits its application to the relation between *probans* and *probandum* in the SP, presumably because in the SP the connection can be taken for granted merely with respect to the realm outside the substratum of inference (*pakṣa*), and

b) that this represents the only legitimate way of using the expression *vyāpti* or related terms.

In the present context it is b) which deserves to be challenged, as shown in the following.

There is 'textual evidence' sustaining the view that terms denoting relations of invariable concomitance are 'domain-neutral' in the sense that they can be applied to pairs of items I_1 and I_2 for which it holds true that with respect to some domain everything exhibiting item I_1 also exhibits item I_2 without imposing any general restrictions concerning the concerned domain, and particularly no limitations to domains which contain the *pakṣa* as an element. In the *Nyāyapraveśa* the terms (edition Dhruva 1968:4,2 and 4,10) i) *sapakṣaikadeśavṛttir vipakṣavyāpī* and ii) *vipakṣaikadeśavṛttiḥ sapakṣavyāpī* appear, denoting fallacious reasons which i) occur in at least one instance of the *sapakṣa*-domain and in all instances of the *vipakṣa*-domain, as e.g. in: 'Sound arises without previous effort because it is non-eternal', ii) occur in at least one instance of the *vipakṣa*-domain and in all instances of the *sapakṣa*-domain, as e.g. in: 'Sound arises after previous effort because it is non-eternal'. The expression *vyatireka-mātravyāpti(ka)*, to be found even in later texts, such as the *Tarkasaṃgraha* and its commentaries (see, e.g. M.R. Bodas 1974:40ff) refers to indicators (*liṅga* = *hetu*) of the so-called *kevala-vyatirekin*-type, where in the realm outside the substratum of inference, such as 'earth' (*pṛthivī*) there are instances exhibiting both absence of the *probans*, such as having smell, and the *probandum*, such as being different from all substances which are not earth, and where everything exhibiting absence of *probandum* exhibits absence of *probans*. In Uddyotakara's *Nyāyavārttika* on *Nyāyasūtra* 1.1.5 and the corresponding section of the *Nyāyabhāṣya* it is said, in the context of a criticism of Buddhist *trairūpya*-doctrines, that, given that one wants to communicate nothing but the mere occurrence of the reason in the realm of similar instances, i.e. instances which are like the *pakṣa* inasmuch as they exhibit the property which the *pakṣa* is claimed to possess (= the *probandum*), this mere occurrence is recognized (by implication) in the form of an occurrence which is undetermined with respect to pervasion or non-pervasion, i.e. which can be either an occurrence in some or in all instances of that realm, on the hypothesis of the satisfaction of the requirement that the reason does not occur specifically in the realm of dissimilar instances.[126]

In the present connection it is the following proposition which possesses primary significance: The supposition

> 1) that terms for invariable concomitance like *vyāpti* and others do not include any general specification concerning domains

and the supposition

> 2) that Dharmakīrti adopted a concept of *vyāpti* according to which exemplification of the *probandum* on the part of the substratum of inference (*pakṣa*) functions as a necessary requirement of the applicability of the term *vyāpti* or related words

are compatible. Even if one grants the contention that a usage of terms of concomitance which do not comply with that concept is legitimate one can still maintain that Dharmakīrti (and some others) employed *vyāpti* in a *meaning* or *sense* which prohibits its application to the relation between *probans* and *probandum* in the SP. The reason can be discerned by considering some more familiar phenomena.

Concerning the concept of the term 'word' the usual distinction between type and token is not the only difference which potentially matters. There are evidently in principle various ways of complying

---

[126] *tattulye ca saṃbhavamātraṃ vivakṣitam iti* | *saṃbhavamātraṃ ca vyāpty-avyāptibhyām* (as in J instead of *vyāptyativyāptibhyām* in A. Thakur 1967:301) *aniyatena saṃbhavena labhyate*.

with the demand of ascertaining the number of word(-token)s on a page. A most straightforward method consists in counting as individual words all units separated by a space. On the other hand, one could also legitimately attempt to fulfil the request by using criteria which take certain grammatical properties into account, such as the possibility to attach markers of inflection, number etc., which could justify the verdict that e.g. 'member care assistant' or 'take off' are to be treated as one unit. Moreover, it could be appropriate to try to comply with some pertinent semantic considerations supporting the decision that, say German '*Pflasterstraße*' counts as a compound of two words as its English equivalent 'cobbled street' disregarding the circumstance that it appears in orthography as a unit without space and that the plural marker '-n' can only be added after the final member. The Spanish expression '*del*' could be regarded as a single word, considering the fact that no internal space occurs in orthography and possibly the circumstance that its meaning could be grasped even without prior consideration of any compositional properties. On the other hand, one might deem relevant that '*del*' is supposed to represent a merger of '*de*' + '*el*' in combination with the fact that the expression possesses a counterpart occurring before feminine nouns which reads '*de la*' so that on the basis of considerations pertaining to linguistic system a treatment of '*del*' as a syntagma could be preferred. Accordingly one could even defend the claim that a word '*del*' does not exist as an element of the (basic) vocabulary of the Spanish language. The upshot is that we should be prepared to accept, apart from the type-token-distinction, a plurality of possible concepts associated with the expression 'word' as well as a plurality of legitimate meanings or senses of that word. In principle, both practical and theoretical considerations should be allowed to come into play, if decisions between different ways of employing the expression need to be made. In accordance with this maxim theoretical innovations constitute a legitimate basis for semantic innovations. In ordinary contexts the word 'sound' is closely associated with the quality of being audible. But presumably theoretical insights into the nature of acoustic phenomena are responsible for a conceptual change permitting expressions, such as ‘ultrasound’, breaking or at least loosening the previous linkbetween ‘sound’ and ‘audibility’.

Despite the dependence of ways of using expressions on contextual factors in the above considered cases one must not conflate them with other phenomena where meaning is or has been supposed to be affected by context. This holds good first and foremost for a phenomenon where a distinction between two (or more) lexical items is ‘contextually neutralized’, which has been discussed in J. Lyons 1968:452[127] and (mis)led the author to hypothesize a ‘context-dependent synonymy’. As a matter of fact, the apparent ‘neutralization’ between the marked term ‘bitch’ and the unmarked term ‘dog’ in a context like

My ___ has just had pups.

is plausibly explained by the hypothesis that ordinary knowledge enables competent speakers to immediately recognize that if ‘My dog has just had pups’ expresses a true proposition then ‘My bitch has just had pups’ would in the same context equally express a true proposition and vice versa. There is no need to assume any context-induced change of meaning or concept regarding ‘dog’ or ‘bitch’ here.

The previously described examples of conceptual change or innovation differ also clearly from cases where expressions containing ‘context-sensitive’, in particular indexical, elements determine a concept on the basis of contextual factors, such as ‘today’s TV-programme’ etc. Expressions of this sort possess some intuitive content that appears to remain invariable in different contexts, but which, by itself, is inapt to determine an extension. The content discernible by a mere linguistic understanding does not enable one to decide which particular TV-programme should be denoted. Accordingly one might distinguish between a ‘notional content’ and a ‘conceptual content’ or differentiate between the terms ‘notion’ and ‘concept’,

---

[127] J. Lyons, *Introduction to Theoretical Linguistics*, Cambridge 1969.

such that the former relates to the relatively invariable component and the latter to a content that is determined, among others by time of utterance, place of utterance and possibly identity of speaker, so that on the basis of those factors information about intended date, country or even channel (first programme, second programme etc.) can be derived. Since even here no compelling need exists to hypothesize changes of meaning, the situation differs from that in the previously considered cases.

It is not merely possible to attribute to Dharmakīrti a *concept* of invariable concomitance which would disallow its applicability to the case of the SP — and to this extent agree to the author of (C) and (E) — but even feasible to provide an explanation for this conceptual innovation that intimately connects it with Dharmakīrti's idea of essential connection, *svabhāvapratibandha*. For someone who has adopted this idea it was natural to suppose that knowledge of the inviolableness of the connection between *probans* and *probandum* could be derived from knowledge about the nature of this connection, viz. that a pertinent relation belongs to the categories of *tadutpatti* or of *tādātmya*. A consequence is that not only the role of 'examples' becomes unessential but that also the need to base the presumption of a general unexceptional concomitance between *probans* and *probandum* on observations to the effect that in some realm the concomitance is nowhere violated is, at least in principle, dispensable. Thus the door is opened for accepting the tenet that a finite being can acquire knowledge to the effect that absolutely every instance of a *probans* must also be an instance of a *probandum* even without having examined a totality of potentially relevant items, i.e. the totality of all objects of the universe where the *probans* is instantiated. In this manner the idea of an absolutely unrestricted pervasion or *vyāpti* attains a completely new status due to the fact that such a connection can be plausibly conceived as an object of possible knowledge on the part of humans or other finite beings. Therefore one can ascertain that thanks to the notion of *svabhāvapratibandha* the theoretical innovations introduced by Dharmakīrti provided a basis for a novel concept of pervasion or *vyāpti*. Without the possibility of referring to *svabhāvapratibandha* any claim to know that an unrestricted invariable concomitance holds good amounted to nothing else than megalomania or hubris. In a framework of earlier theories like that of Vasubandhu one could at best claim that due to a definite ascertainment of an invariable connection in some examined domain one possesses good reason to presume that the connection is never violated in the entire realm apart from the substratum of inference and on the basis of that presumption to suppose a non-violation of this regularity with respect to the *pakṣa*. Hence a concept of unrestricted *vyāpti* is not congenial to the older framework inasmuch as it cannot be plausibly conceived as an object of possible knowledge.

In response to the possible objection that no (textual) evidence exists to the effect that theoreticians before Dharmakīrti carried out contemplations along the above portrayed lines and developed a concept of pervasion optimally fitting their own theoretical framework the following deserves to be said:

1. There is, as far as one can see, no similar evidence with respect to such contemplations on the part of Dharmakīrti either, so that even contentions concerning Dharmakīrti's concept of *vyāpti* must rely on other sources than explicit considerations or discussions about the most suitable shape of the idea.

2. In the light of the deliberations of the previous paragraph it must be deemed improper to dismiss from the outset assessments pertaining to suitability and reasonability as irrelevant.

3. The thesis advocated in the present connection does not entail that a specific and determinate concept of pervasion or invariable concomitance had been elaborated before Dharmakīrti. To be sure, it does not militate against this assumption. On the other hand, however, it seems quite probable that authors alluding to a knowledge of invariable concomitance like in Vasubandhu's

illustrious definition of inference[128] left room for a certain amount of indeterminateness regarding the nature of the pertinent knowledge: Whereas it can be safely ruled out that knowledge of an infallible connection between *probans* and *probandum* should not be a knowledge resting, among other things, on the observation that both items are exemplified by the substratum of inference — because of the supposition that inferences ordinarily lead to the acquisition of new knowledge — it is easily conceivable that no definite view had been developed regarding the query of the extension of the domain where an invariable concomitance is to be definitely ascertained, leaving room for the alternatives a) that the ascertainment pertains to some or the other (finite) domain, b) that the ascertainment pertains to the entire domain outside the substratum of inference, c) that the ascertainment pertains to the entire domain in so far as it *can* have been scrutinized before by someone who undertakes an inference. Given that an author has not, at least for himself, explicitly differentiated between the different options, his statements containing references to some knowledge can only be treated like 'templates' confronting an interpreter with the task of filling the blanks in such a way that an explication is obtained which i) possesses the best chances of representing a truth or ii) renders the making of the statement most reasonable against the background of the attitudes adopted by the proponent, specifically his beliefs and desires. This is a situation which often occurs if linguistic items containing vague terms are to be assessed.[129]

---

[128] *nāntarīyakārthadarśanaṃ tadvido 'numānam.*

[129] Situations of this kind are frequent because items containing vague expressions as constituents can be used in a way which implies a demand directed at addressees or potential interpreters to identify themselves some explication which yields a content that can be assessed as true and which renders a pertinent linguistic act most reasonable against the background of its context. Someone who utters in an assertive mode the sentence

Tom is rich.

The connection between quantifiers, in particular universal quantifiers, and domain-restrictions is a well-known phenomenon. It is easy to see that a sentence like

(I) All adults pay income tax.

can be used to state various things in accordance with specific domains constituting the topic of a discourse, such as some group of workers, working people in general, citizens of a particular country or group of countries, human-beings living in present-day societies etc. On the other hand, it is not inconsistent with the meaning of quantifiers like 'every' or 'all' to employ them without any domain-restriction at all. Presumably more often in theoretical than in everyday contexts universal statements occur which could be properly represented by using variables whose range pertains to types or categories of objects like physical events or other physical objects, natural numbers or numbers in general and in a limiting case even to entities of any category. It is this fact which permits to convert even ordinary statements embodying domain-restrictions into statements represented by more complex formulations allowing to dispense with the original restrictions, such as:

---

will presumably not intend to make a demand on the addressee that he should accept his statement as true without further consideration. However — at least as long as the addressee is not supposed to be a linguist or (analytic) philosopher of language — the communicative intention goes usually far beyond the question of the truth of the item considered in isolation. Presuming rationality on the part of the speaker an interpreter possessing suitable information about context can ascertain that the communicatively relevant goal consists in imparting, for example, the message that the person referred to in the utterance is rich enough to buy an apartment in the city of London, or that under prevailing circumstances no need exists to provide financial help or that an attitude of arrogance exhibited by a person called 'Tom' can be explained etc. If the linguistic content of the uttered sentence is embedded in such contexts the vagueness inherent in the lexical meaning of 'rich' becomes irrelevant and focusing on the complex communicative content an interpreter might assess it as definitely true or untrue, in accordance with the circumstances.

All adults working in the YMCA pay income tax.
All adults, if/in so far as they work in the YMCA, pay income tax.[130]

etc. Thus one can ascertain the existence of a contrast between a) a linguistic meaning of linguistic items containing quantifiers as constituents which is completely indeterminate with respect to domain-restrictions not merely regarding the identity of the relevant domain but even with respect to the existence or absence of a domain-restriction at all[131] and b) a content which is specified either by reference to some specific domain or by the absence of any domain-restriction. As far as assessments of truth or untruth are concerned, it is evidently the second variety which matters. Presumably — and some persons might say, hopefully — (I) represents a falsehood if the quantification is interpreted without domain-restriction. Given that the linguistic meaning of items containing quantifiers due to its neutrality with respect to domain-restriction is not assessable in terms of definite truth or untruth although it plays a palpable role in the process of mapping linguistic units to contents which are assessable in this way, one is entitled to characterize the relatively invariant content

---

[130] These statements can be completely appropriate, given that in the pertinent organization also non-adult persons perform jobs which are by law exempt from taxes.

[131] One could be tempted to assimilate the two varieties of universal quantifications with domain-restrictions and quantifications without them by hypothesizing references to domains in their (underlying) general form, i.e. by analysing 'every ....' as 'every .... in (domain) D', 'all ....' as 'all .... in (domain) D' etc., and to interpret non-restricted quantifications as quantifications resulting by universal quantifications over domains. The crux is, however, that in this way novel quantifications appear on the scene which themselves raise issues of domain-restriction. — Compared with this account even the supposition of an ambiguity between quantifications with and quantifications without domain-restrictions appears preferable. However, in the present context those details can be disregarded.

associated with the (standing) meaning of sentences like (I) by the term 'propositional template'.[132]

Considering against this background the relationship between a concomitance or pervasion which is determined with respect to the inclusion of a substratum of inference and a kind of pervasion that is not determined in this regard one can ascertain that the former relates to the latter as a proposition to a proposition-template. A concept of pervasion implying an absolutely unrestricted concomitance between *probans* and *probandum* contrasts with an idea of infallible concomitance permitting restriction to some particular domain in the manner in which a linguistic meaning of an item containing quantifiers as ingredients contrasts with a proposition which definitely rules out

---

[132] This is not the only option to account for the pertinent facts. An alternative possibility is to correlate with linguistic meanings of items containing universal quantifiers universal propositions not restricted to any domain. Considering the circumstance that it is not reasonable for a speaker to assert such propositions under given circumstances (under which they are blatantly false) one disregards their truth-evaluation and assesses the concerned statements exclusively with respect to domain-restricted correlates which can be identified by taking contextual features into account. Consequently, apart from a propositional content that is definitely false another propositional content is communicated which might turn out to be true or untrue according to the actual circumstances. Presuming that it is only the latter content whose truth a speaker intends to claim interpreters will consider its truth or untruth for deciding whether they should agree or disagree with an assertion. Two points matter in the present connection: 1) Preferring the second account with respect to (complex) linguistic units containing explicit universal quantifiers is in principle compatible with adopting the first alternative with respect to units where universal quantifications occur as integral components of the meaning of individual words; accordingly it could still hold good that expressions, such as *vyāpti* and other related terms, possess a standing linguistic meaning which exhibits indeterminacy with respect to domain-restriction or, as elements of the linguistic system, stand for concept-templates that can be implemented by concepts where the neutrality regarding domain-restriction is abolished, like, supposedly, by Dharmakīrti's concept of *vyāpti*. 2) Even under the second alternative view it holds good that identical linguistic items are to be correlated with different contents and types of meaning at the same time and for the derivation of contents which matter for verdicts about truth or untruth considerations of reasonability must play a vital role.

any domain-restriction. Accordingly one is entitled to make an analogous distinction between 'concept' and 'concept-template', so that even the hypothesis that Dharmakīrti or others adopted some concept of pervasion or *vyāpti* disallowing its application in the case of the SP is compatible with the supposition of a corresponding concept-template that does not exhibit this feature and which is more intimately linked to the lexical or linguistic meaning of pertinent terms. It is, however, neither necessary nor appropriate to content oneself with this result. One can go much further, as the following shows.

A concept of pervasion implying an unrestricted pervasion between *probans* and *probandum* can be plausibly regarded as the outcome of a specific 'semantic enrichment' resulting from a replacement of the idea of a pervasion by the idea of a pervasion which can be definitely ascertained. Given the presupposition of an ascertainable essential connection, i.e. a *svabhāvapratibandha*, a basis existed for the supposition that compliance with an unrestricted pervasion can be definitely ascertained even without surveillance of the entire universe. To be sure, the question of whether or not Dharmakīrti was objectively entitled to adopt this belief in the way he did is an entirely different matter. Anyhow, in the framework of theories lacking the idea of essential connection no similar ground existed for deriving such a bold conclusion, but on the other hand, there was a solid basis for the tenet that infallible concomitance relations can be definitely ascertained in specific domains that do not include the substratum of inference, the so-called *pakṣa*. It is a specific 'merit' of the SP that it makes evident on the one hand, that a definite ascertainment of compliance with an infallible concomitance is not merely possible with respect to some or the other domain but even with respect to the entire domain apart from the substratum of inference and that an argument, despite of exhibiting this feature, might nevertheless fail. There is no reason to call into question the assumption that the creator(s) of the SP *intentionally* designed the example in such a way that the infallible connection between *probans* and *probandum* in the entire non-*pakṣa* domain is absolutely undeniable. This holds good not only on the assumption that the SP was meant to perform a 'critical' function but also on the supposition that it should establish a 'materialist' tenet.

It is precisely this important fact which had been concealed in the portrayal of (A), and in particular by the remarks that it is an 'unfounded assumption ... that the Cārvāka attempts to establish a vyāpti', that 'there is no concomitance between the reason and the property to be proved' as well as recommendations to the effect that we should not attribute 'to the Cārvāka unconvincing attempts to establish a concomitance where there is none' and that we ought to 'stop looking at the Cārvāka inference through *vyāpti*-glasses' (p. 221). On the other hand it turns out that the statement made in (B) that 'raising the question of whether or not the advocates of the *sadvitīyaprayoga* attempted to establish a concomitance or *vyāpti* .... can be misleading' because 'in some sense at least, the postulate of an invariable concomitance should be satisfied by arguments of the *sadvitīya*-type' requires an explication, which could read as follows:

> There is a linguistically conveyed notion or concept-template of invariable concomitance which a) permits an application to the SP and b) whose implementation by a concept of *vyāpti* supposedly adopted by Dharmakīrti disallows an application to the SP. The latter concept can be understood as being developed against the background of a theory that attributes to *svabhāvapratibandha* a function for the ascertainment of an invariable concomitance between *probans* and *probandum* via a semantic enrichment replacing the notion of invariable concomitance by a notion of ascertainable invariable concomitance. On the other hand, concepts of *vyāpti* are applicable to the SP, such that the advocates of the SP intended their satisfaction. They exhibit the following qualities: i) they implement the notion or concept-template of invariable concomitance, ii) they are mediated by a similar semantic enrichment as in the former case and iii) they accord with a theoretical framework where *svabhāvapratibandha* and its ascertainment do not possess any function. Those conditions are met by α) an invariable concomitance between *probans* and *probandum* in some

domain outside the *pakṣa* or β) an invariable concomitance in the entire non-*pakṣa* domain.

This explication is admittedly intricate. However, against the contention that the complexity discredits the account, the following deserves to be retorted: The series of claims advanced in (A) require a complex explication too, if they should represent an acceptable tenet. Such an explication could run as follows:

> The creator(s) of the SP did not intend that the relation between the *probans* and *probandum* in the SP should comply with a concept of invariable concomitance. This concept is identical with the conception of *vyāpti* that had been adopted by Dharmakīrti. It results by an implementation of the notion corresponding to the linguistic meaning of the term against the background of a theory attributing to *svabhāvapratibandha* a function for the assessment of an invariable concomitance between *probans* and *probandum* via a semantic enrichment replacing the notion of invariable concomitance by a notion of ascertainable invariable concomitance.

Both explications are more complex than any of the corresponding formulations appearing in (A) or in (B), but they make manifest that there is no imperative necessity to assess positions as incompatible which can appear irreconcilable. Among the consequences which might be drawn from the above presented assessment of the situation two deserve to be mentioned in the first place:

1. Increase of explicitness tends to entail the disadvantage of increasing complexity and a corresponding loss of economy of expression. However, the gain of economization in the short run can be counterbalanced by a loss of economy in a longer run. Dedicating more space to the exposition of a subject matter in the first article could have prevented the composition of subsequent treatises dealing with the topic. If the authors of (A) as well as of (B) had in the very beginning exposed their views with more clarity and explicitness the feeling of a need to correct misunderstandings might not have arisen

at all. Even if members engaged in a dispute might themselves fail to discern the actual state of affairs, explication is conducive to a better assessment on the part of impartial observers. It is appropriate to highlight this truism because it appears that ideologies as well as prevailing institutional conditions do not facilitate expositions revealing the complexities of a matter.

2. Irrespective of whether or not concepts of concomitance or *vyāpti* had been adopted at certain times which could not be correctly applied to the argument of the SP, the fact persists that a distinction between linguistically imparted contents on the one hand and concepts on the other hand needs to be taken into consideration. To be sure, the difference is most patent with respect to linguistic items containing indexical elements as constituents. But it appears erroneous to suppose that the existence of this disparity is confined to that realm. The parallelism is significant enough even to justify the employment of the terms 'notion' and 'concept' for signalling differences in the domain of expressions not containing overt indexical elements, notwithstanding the circumstance that they entered the scene in connection with syntagmas, such as 'today's TV-programme'. But there is an important difference too: In the case of determinations of various contents in accordance with variations of contextual features due to the 'context-sensitivity' of linguistic elements no plausible basis exists for hypothesizing any divergences of sense or meaning; there is on the one hand a stable linguistic sense and on the other hand a plurality of contents determined by relevant qualities of context. The situation is different in the case of implementations of notions or 'conceptual templates' by diverse concepts; a possibly invariant meaning imparted by linguistic conventions contrasts with possibly[133] diverse meanings

[133] The expression 'possibly' is added here to account for the theoretical possibility that in the history of a language a notion or concept-template has been implemented only once by a concept; if, for example, the only concept of concomitance apt for the precise determination of extensions had been elaborated by Dharmakīrti as it is represented by *his* conception of *vyāpti*.

corresponding to various concepts. Presumably this conception of a meaning that is on the one hand linked up with a lexical meaning of linguistic expressions although it cannot be uniquely derived from it (not even in combination of contextual features) and on the other hand uniquely associated with concepts is closely related to the idea of 'restricted meaning' as explained in Hattiangadi 1987:62ff.[134]

It might be demurred that the idea is not entirely novel and that it had been anticipated even in the field of traditional philologies, as evidenced by titles of studies of the form 'the concept of X in Y', 'der Begriff von X bei Z', where 'X' is replaced by the designation of a linguistic expression, 'Y' be the name of a text or work and 'Z' by the name of a person. Nevertheless the contention that those observations vindicate an insight in the matter is at best a half-truth. On the one hand titles of this kind intimate the absence of an awareness of the facts i) that expressions can possess different 'restricted meanings' for one and the same person in different contexts and ii) that even different occurrences of identical terms in one and the same text might be associated with different concepts and that such situations are by no means exceptional.[135] On the other hand an intuitive awareness of the phenomenon does not guarantee a clear recognition of the consequences which can be validly derived from its occurrence in individual cases. The latter point possesses special importance. It is true that even without a theoretical background it might be feasible to ascertain that, say, Dharmakīrti adopted a concept of pervasion requiring the actual

---

[134] J.N. Hattiangadi 1987.

[135] The previously considered example of determining word-units in diverse ways by different criteria is apt to bring this point home. Applied to standard examples of vague expressions, such as 'bald', 'tall', 'rich', 'heap' etc., the account implying a contrast between relatively invariant lexical meanings as well as concept-templates on the one hand and a plurality of restricted meanings and concepts on the other is apt to offer an explanation of the fact that, as far as one can see, all natural languages are replete with vague terms. The explanation reads as follows: It is advantageous for a linguistic system if it provides the possibility to generate a countless number of concepts by means of a limited vocabulary.

exemplification of a *probandum* by a substratum of inference which would not permit its correct application to the argument of the SP, as long as the existence of bodies possessing consciousness is not established. The crucial point lies however in the question as to what can be deduced from this fact. The problem lies in the validity of arguments derived from possibly correct observations. It is relevant specifically for the contention that the advocates of the SP did not attempt to comply with *any* form of concomitance given that they could not satisfy a concept of pervasion adopted by Dharmakīrti. Disclaiming the importance of higher-order reflections on the soundness of conclusions to be drawn from observations destroys the fundament of any science. If the lack of self-criticism favoured by this attitude affects a larger group in a field, a collective self-aggrandizement standing in sharp contrast to the actual state of affairs is a most probable outcome.

IV

The author of (E) claims, p. 531, that if his works would be read attentively, one would never think that he considered the word *anyatara* to refer only to an exclusive disjunction and presents as reason the fact that he had before written a passage which reads as follows:

> However, when Dharmakīrti says *sāmānyena* ('in general') as in *sādhyaṃ sāmānyena saṃmatam* (PV 4.34), *sāmānyena sādhyam iṣṭam iti na viśeṣāpekṣaḥ* (PVin III 14.9) or similar expressions, he probably simply means that the disjunction should be taken as inclusive 'or', i.e., is considered true if the one, the other or both its members are true, disregarding whether it is the one or the other 'particular' (i.e., the person or the pot).

This is an odd argument. The writer of (E) obviously thinks that his statement that Dharmakīrti believes that the disjunction (represented by *anyatara*) should be taken as an inclusive 'or' provides conclusive evidence for the fact that he himself believes that the disjunction should be taken as an inclusive 'or'. This is extremely odd because statements of the form 'B believes that C means D', or 'B says that C means D' made on the part of A suggest, by conversational implicatures à la Grice, that the utterer, i.e. A, does himself *not* believe that C means D or regards such a supposition as questionable. To be sure, if 'B' is substituted by 'the bible' and 'A' stands for an expression denoting a devout Christian, it might be indeed appropriate to draw from a corresponding statement of the form 'B says that C means D' the conclusion that A himself believes that C means that D. But unfortunately the writer of (E) did not disclose beforehand that he had become a Dharmakīrti devotee. Nevertheless, it is not needed to pursue the issue further because there are other things which matter more in the present connection.

In (C), p. 669, the following passage occurs:

> Both authors (of the *sadvitīyaprayoga* and *pakṣasapakṣānyataratva* argument) used what one may call an "alternating disjunction." The word *anyatara* means "(only) one of the two", but the trick in their usage of the word is that it is not always the same one (this use of the disjunction gets lost in Oetke's annotations and formalizations). In the latter case, when the first *trairūpya* condition is examined, the left side of the disjunction holds true, when the second condition is examined, the right.

To this a footnote is added which reads as follows:

> In the *sadvitīyaprayoga*, on the other hand, the alternation is between the *sādhyadharma* and the *sapakṣa*. Note, however, that the alternation occurs only for the opponent. For the proponent, the disjunction in the *sapakṣa* is not exclusive, since he accepts the existence of both the pot and the materialistic person.

Although the quoted passage follows immediately after some statements about Dharmakīrti's intentions and concerns, its topic evidently relates to the import of *anyatara* as used by the advocates of the *sadvitīyaprayoga*- and of the *pakṣasapakṣānyataratva*-arguments.

In the light of the last sentence of the quoted passage of the main text, viz. 'In the latter case ....', one can ascertain that the so-called '*pakṣasapakṣānyataratva*-argument' exhibits the characteristic feature that it employs a disjunctive *probans* whose individual members cannot be instantiated together by any object (of the universe). For, given that the domains of *pakṣa* and of *sapakṣa* are separate, the *pakṣa* can only exhibit the property of being a/the *pakṣa* (in the pertinent context of inference), whereas all remaining entities of the universe can at most, provided they exemplify the property of being eternal (since being eternal is supposed to constitute the *probandum*), exhibit the property of being (a) *sapakṣa* (relative to the context of inference). All other items must be neither *pakṣa* nor *sapakṣa*. Hence the first *trairūpya*-condition stipulating that the substratum of inference = *pakṣa* is satisfied by the fact that the *pakṣa* exhibits precisely the first member of the disjunction. The second requirement, according to which in the realm of 'similar instances' = *sapakṣa* at least one item exists that exhibits both *probans* and *probandum*, is satisfied by the existence of any entity which is both eternal and *sapakṣa*, but no item that is both eternal and *pakṣa* can fulfil this function, given that the realms of *pakṣa* and *sapakṣa* are separate. For that reason the *pakṣasapakṣānyataratva*-argument possesses validity by the criterion of *trairūpya* only on condition that eternal objects exist at all. The remaining requirement, that every object exhibiting the *probans* exhibits the *probandum* too, is trivially satisfied in the *sapakṣa*-realm because relative to the pertinent context of inference this realm is determined as a realm of objects whose members exhibit the quality of being eternal without any exception. Nevertheless, the proposition that the *pakṣa* exhibits the quality of being eternal too is not automatically guaranteed by the circumstance that every item belonging to the *sapakṣa*-domain must be eternal. Therefore a compliance with the conditions of *trairūpya* can never *entail* the truth of the thesis, at least as long as *pakṣa* and *sapakṣa* are considered as constituting separate realms.

In the light of the final sentence of the corresponding footnote, viz. 'For the proponent ....', it can be recognised that an advocate of the *sadvitīyaprayoga*-argument who takes the existence of material bodies endowed with consciousness for granted, would believe that both constituents of the disjunctive *probandum* are exhibited by members belonging to the *sapakṣa*-realm, such as chairs, trees, mushrooms or even computers, all of which differ both from pots and from conscious bodies. But for everybody who does not take the existence of material bodies endowed with consciousness for granted the situation is different: All objects of the *sapakṣa*-realm are bound to exhibit the second component of the disjunction, viz. being different from a/the pot, given, as before, the separateness of the *pakṣa*- and *sapakṣa*-domains, whereas the exemplification of the remaining member is open to doubt. On the other hand, the *pakṣa* can evidently not exhibit the quality of being different from *pakṣa*, so that it can at most exhibit the other member of the disjunction; but given that the existence of conscious bodies is not taken for granted, not even this can be regarded as certain. So far there is no problem.

A first, but perhaps not decisive, difficulty arises due to the contention that '[i]n the *sadvitīyaprayoga* .... the alteration is between the *sādhyadharma* and the *sapakṣa*'. The difficulty is not merely due to the circumstance that it has not been made explicit what, in the eyes of the writer, should be considered as *sādhyadharma* and as *sapakṣa* respectively. The crux is rather that a disjunction between something which could be identified as *probandum* = *sādhyadharma* on the one hand and something which could be plausibly considered as *sapakṣa* nowhere occurs in the SP. Given that the *sādhyadharma* consists itself in the disjunctive quality of being different from (a) conscious body or being different from (a) pot, it can hardly be a member of any 'alternating disjunction' and thus even less a constituent of an alternating disjunction between *sādhyadharma* and *sapakṣa*. The *sapakṣa*, on the other hand, should be a realm to which all objects belong which are (either) different from conscious bodies or different from certain pots and it remains unclear why this realm — or any realm of objects at all — are to be considered as an ingredient of an alternating disjunction. Up to now, at best the following conjecture can be offered: Presuming that the SP is advocated by a materialist, the writer of the above quoted passages considered exclusively the property of differing from conscious bodies as the 'genuine' *probandum*; and considering that differing from a pot is a necessary condition of being a (member of the) *sapakṣa*(-realm) the expression *sapakṣa* has been employed for referring to this property. Be this as it may, it is hardly disputable that the properties of differing from a conscious body and the property of differing from a pot are the only items which could, in the context of the SP, play a role which is analogous to the role played by the properties of being *pakṣa* and of being *sapakṣa* in the context of the *pakṣasapakṣānyataratva*-argument, so that further deliberations concerning the peculiar way of designating them might be dispensable.

The crucial question is: Why did the writer claim that the authors of the SP and of the *pakṣasapakṣānyataratva*-argument *used* a disjunction which might be called 'alternating disjunction' and why is it remarked that this use of the disjunction gets lost in particular formalizations? One should think that if somebody utters in an assertive mode:

(II) Everybody in this area owns a BMW or a Mercedes.

he uses the disjunction in exactly the same manner irrespective of whether or not the actual situation happens to be so that some of the residents in the concerned area own both a BMW and a Mercedes. One might demur that in the cases of the SP and the *pakṣasapakṣānyataratva*-argument the members of the disjunctions do not merely happen to be satisfied by different items; rather it is possible to ascertain in advance that no object can satisfy both members together, at least under certain presuppositions. But in cases, such as

(III) All numbers in the set consisting of 6, 9, 12 and 15 can be divided by 3 or 5.

on the one hand and

> (III*) All numbers in the set consisting of 6, 9, 10 and 12 can be divided by 3 or 5.

on the other hand, it is equally obvious that, whereas in the first case one of the numbers can be divided by both 3 and by 5, in the second case all numbers can be divided by either 3 or by 5 but no number exists which is divisible by both 3 and 5. Why should it be claimed that in (III) and in (III*) the disjunctions are used in different ways and that (III*) is distinguished by the use of an alternating disjunction? One can leave aside the query, what the writer of (C) has in mind when he speaks of 'formalizations' and whether it would refer to formalizations in a genuine sense of the term or rather to representations of some content by means of expressions taken from Symbolic Logic. In either case the question must be raised as to why some use of a disjunction 'gets lost' in particular formalizations and why it is significant to register this alleged loss. Does not, for example,

> All numbers in the set S can be divided by X or Y.

provide a suitable formalization for both (III) and (III*)? Even considering the fact that identical items usually permit different formalizations representing different ways or levels of abstraction, no plausible reason exists to treat (III) and (III*) differently in this respect. For the difference between those units does not pertain to their syntactic or semantic form but to the circumstance that different substitutions for 'S' yield items which are true or false under different circumstances. If, on the other hand, (explicating) paraphrases employing devices borrowed from Symbolic Logic are at stake, it would be appropriate to render both (III) and (III*) by a formulation, such as:

> (∀x)(x ε {6, 9, 12,15 }   (x can be divided by 3 v x can be divided by 5))

for (III) and

$(\forall x)(x \in \{6, 9, 10, 12\}$ (x can be divided by 3 v x can be divided by 5))

for (III*) would be permissible. The only difference pertains to the specification of the members of the pertinent sets. This is sufficient for providing the information needed for a recognition of the fact that in contrast to (III) the members of the set in (III*) can all be divided by either 3 or 5 but no member could be divided by both numbers. Both a genuine formalization and a 'symbolic paraphrase' would call for a reflection of a difference with respect to the nature of disjunction only if the meaning or sense of the disjunctive terms, i.e. the occurrences of 'or' in the two sentences, were different.

On the other hand however, the supposition that the disjunctive term in (III*) should not be taken in the sense of an inclusive disjunction and that (III) and (III*) might be represented by different kinds of disjunctions is not absurd. For if the disjunction of (III*) would be interpreted in the sense of a disjunction currently termed 'exclusive disjunction' (III*) would express a truth too.

One could indeed argue that, since i) in the above quoted passage instead of the usual term 'exclusive disjunction' the expression 'alternating disjunction' appears and ii) it was remarked that the alternation occurs only for the opponent and not for the proponent, one ought to conclude that nodifferent type of disjunction had been envisaged. But in view of the facts

a) that the text speaks of a use of 'alternating disjunction'

b) that it intimates that annotations and specific 'formalizations' relying on the assumption that the SP as well as the *pakṣasapakṣānyataratva*-argument employ an inclusive disjunction do not impart what they ought to impart

c) that the immediately preceding sentence expresses the assertion that 'Dharmakīrti's arguments concern mainly the nature of the disjunction', in combination with the circumstance

d) that an interpretation of *anyatara* as signalling an exclusive disjunction appears to represent the only possibility to justify the assumption that the SP as well as the *pakṣasapakṣānyataratva*-argument employ a special type of disjunction where the disjunctive operator does not possess the sense of an inclusive 'or'

a circumspective interpreter has hardly any other choice than to consider as a realistic possibility the intention to contend that the disjunctions in the concerned arguments possess an exclusive nature. Even if the question of intention were disregarded it would be unwarranted to omit a critical inspection of the query as to whether an employment of exclusive disjunctions in the pertinent arguments could be a reasonable option. Maybe, the examination yielding as a result that by using an exclusive disjunction in the SP a satisfying argument is not obtainable was irrelevant inasmuch the writer of (C) never intended to claim that the disjunction is exclusive. But if that is the case the pertinent point has been depicted in an inappropriate manner. A portrayal of the situation in a form that is decisively more suitable could read as follows:

Both the *sadvitīyaprayoga* and the *pakṣasapakṣānyataratva*-argument exhibit the characteristic that, at least under certain presuppositions, no object can instantiate both terms of the disjunctions. For in the case of the *pakṣasapakṣānyataratva*-argument the *probans* can be exhibited by the *pakṣa* only due to the circumstance that it exhibits, and even must exhibit, the first member of the disjunction, viz. the property of being *pakṣa,* whereas an exemplification of the other member of the disjunction is impossible (given that the domains of *pakṣa* and *sapakṣa* are separate). All the remaining objects of the universe can at most exemplify the second member of the disjunction, which they in fact exhibit if they instantiate the property of being eternal. Hence the first condition of *trairūpya* is satisfied because the *pakṣa* must exhibit the first member of the disjunction, whereas the second condition of *trairūpya* can be satisfied at best due to the exemplification of the second member on the part of an eternal item that is not the *pakṣa* itself. All this can be ascertained beforehand, without investigating contingent matters of the world. In the case of the *sadvitīyaprayoga* the *probandum* is such that its exhibition on the part of the *pakṣa* as well as its exhibition by some items belonging to the *sapakṣa*-realm would be guaranteed if the existence of physical bodies endowed with consciousness were taken as granted. The disjunctive property would be exhibited by the *pakṣa* due to the fact that it exhibits the property of being different from some conscious body; a number of items in the *sapakṣa*-domain would exhibit both properties because they differ both from some pot or some collection of pots (functioning as *pakṣa*) and from some conscious body. If, however, the existence of physical bodies of consciousness were not taken for granted or if it is even denied (as an opponent would presumably do), then the exemplification of the second member on the part of certain elements of the *sapakṣa*-realm would be guaranteed due to the fact that they must be different from any pot that functions as *pakṣa*; but regarding the *pakṣa* itself an exhibition of the second member of the disjunction is impossible and an exemplification of the other member is at best doubtful. This state of affairs can be equally assessed in advance without investigating contingent circumstances. Although the pertinent characteristic peculiarities are not and should not be made manifest in formalizations of the arguments they were regarded as fatal flaws by Dharmakīrti.

In answer to the possible criticism that the recasting is considerably longer than the original depiction presented in (C) the following facts deserve to be pointed out:

1) The rewritten portrayal shines a light on additional details due to its greater explicitness.

2) It does not suggest that in the SP and the *pakṣasapakṣānyataratva*-argument a special type of disjunction enters the scene.

3) It does not intimate mistaken conclusions concerning the function of formalizations or explications employing symbolic notations.

4) It provides a palpable indication of the presumable ground in virtue of which Dharmakīrti considered the two pieces of reasoning reproachable and permits to clearly identify a maxim postulated for acceptable pieces of inference or proof. The relevant maxim is: Whenever a specimen of inference or proof contains a disjunctive *probans* or *probandum* it must not be ascertainable from the outset that one (or more) members of the disjunction cannot be instantiated by the substratum of inference, i.e. the item that functions as *pakṣa* in the pertinent context. Thereby it is tacitly admitted that in a wider field of inferences, where qualities functioning as *probans* or *probandum* might exhibit (among others) a disjunctive form, the canon of *trairūpya* can only work if the doctrine is complemented by additional restrictions. It is against the background of this novel postulate that one could address further questions regarding the justifiability of Dharmakīrti's stance.[136]

---

[136] A problem is caused by the fact that the complex character of a predicate is not necessarily exhibited by its linguistic form. Dispositional qualities represented by atomic adjectives like '[x is] brittle' or '[x is] (water-)soluble' are sometimes claimed to be equivalent or even 'reducible' to properties representable by complex expressions, such as '[x] dissolves if [x were] put in water'. But even most ordinary words or predicates like '[x is a] child' can be regarded as being equivalent to words or predicates exhibiting a disjunctive form, such as '[x is a] boy or [x is a] girl'. Should accordingly an inference using being a child as a *probandum* be illegitimate in situations where it can be ascertained from the outset that the 'substratum of inference' must be male — or female, as the case may be? If this consequence would be accepted, it would become imperative to accept a postulate according to which a *probans* or a *probandum* of an inference must always be the most specific property in the sense that it cannot be considered as equivalent to a disjunctive quality of the form '[x is] Q or Q*', where it could be ascertained in advance that one member of the disjunction — 'Q' or 'Q*' — is not exhibited by the substratum of inference. Against the possible demurral that the adoption of such a theorem is not attested in texts written by Dharmakīrti or by writers of the subsequent tradition, the following reply deserves to be given: Does not precisely this circumstance vindicate that a fatal impoverishment results from the precept 'to understand a tradition in its own terms' if this implies the

It emerges again that increase of elaborateness and explicitness can be conducive to economy in the longer run by making disputes rooted in unclarities about interpretation dispensable. For the same reason the relevance of paying more attention to accuracy in matters of formulation deserves to be emphasized. Such points possess particular importance in disciplines which due to peculiarities of their definition and delimitation are affected by an immanent propensity to favour communicability and convenience at the expense of precision and depth.

V

(D) is affected by two shortcomings which deserve to be revealed. Since the concerned matters have not yet been properly clarified and the possibility that they fall into oblivion is not unrealistic, this self-criticism appears apposite. Initially the first issue could seem peripheral considering the circumstance that it pertains to a relation between the SP and some other doctrinal element. But due to the existence of implications relating to potential argumentative functions of this specimen of reasoning it cannot be justified to pass the point over in silence.

In (D), p. 509, it had been contended that it has not (yet) been conclusively refuted that 'to establish the "materialist" tenet that persons are nothing but bodies manifesting phenomena of consciousness' was 'an originally intended purpose' of the reasoning presented in the SP and that 'the mere circumstance that ... the argument must be regarded as faulty because it can be 'counterbalanced' by a parallel argument establishing the very opposite fulfilling exactly the same criteria of validity' cannot disprove this supposition, viz. the hypothesis that the SP was originally connected with the intention to establish a central tenet of

maxim to disregard all properties of a teaching which had not been recognized by its creator or the subsequent tradition of its reception?

materialism. To support the contention it was remarked that 'there is no conclusive evidence showing that the original proponents were acquainted with the concept of *viruddhāvyabhicāra'* and that the doctrinal element of *viruddhāvyabhicāra* could have even been created as a reaction facing the problem of the SP. The major fault does not lie in the contention itself but in the manner in which it had been endorsed by a consideration pertaining to the *viruddhāvyabhicāra.*

Against the supposition that some creator of the SP, who was not acquainted with the idea of *viruddhāvyabhicāra,* wanted to prove a tenet of materialism by the piece of reasoning which the SP represents, the writer of (E) = FN quite rightly objects, p. 528, that 'even if the author of the sp were not aware of the concept of *viruddhāvyabhicāra*, it would still be ludicrous to assume that he believed that he could actually prove the materialistic Lokāyata tenet with it'. The reason is that 'it is obvious .... that if the sp is valid, the following is equally valid: The pot is accompanied by a pot or by an eternal soul, because it is not a lotus, etc.' Nevertheless, this treatment of the issue fails to get to the root of the matter.

First, any satisfactory identification of the exact nature of the relationship between the situation of counterbalancing the SP by a parallel argument attempting to establish a contrary tenet and the situation envisaged in the *viruddhāvyabhicāra* is nowhere presented in the entire dispute represented by (A)–(E). For there are striking differences. The pertinent situation in the case of the *viruddhāvyabhicāra* is characterized by a presentation of pairs of reasoning trying to incompatible *probanda* with respect to the same substratum of inference (*pakṣa*), such that each of which employs a different *probans*. In the *Nyāyapraveśa* the situation is illustrated by the two pairs: 'Sound is impermanent because it is produced like a pot; sound is permanent because it is audible like [the universal] sound-ness'. [137]

[137] *viruddhāvyabhicārī yathā* | *anityaḥ śabdaḥ kṛtakatvād ghaṭavat* | *nityaḥ śabdaḥ śrāvaṇatvāt śabdatvavad iti* | *ubhayoḥ saṃśayahetutvād dvāv apy etāv eko 'naikāntikaḥ samuditāv eva* | (Edition Dhruva 1968:4,21–5,2).

Notwithstanding possible uncertainties of interpretation in detail it can be definitely ascertained that the *viruddhāvyabhicāra* relates to cases where conflicting results are licensed (to the same degree) by pieces of reasoning resorting to different specimens of *probans*. Those cases are evidently connected with the phenomenon of 'conflicting evidence'. In the case of the SP, however, a situation is envisaged which is *not* characterized by an exploitation of conflicting evidence. It is rather supposed that one-and-the same *probans* is employed for establishing different *probanda* which are 'logically compatible' in so far as there are entities which could exemplify the pertinent *probanda* at the same time: Obviously items which are not pots themselves could exhibit both the quality of differing from some pot or differing from conscious bodies as well as the quality of differing from some pot or differing from bodies endowed with souls which (i.e. the souls) alone are bearers of consciousness (granted that the disjunction is inclusive). Only the idea of attributing both *probanda* to a pot, functioning as *pakṣa*, creates difficulties – *provided* it is hypothesized in addition that it cannot be true that some entities exist whose physical bodies are endowed with consciousness and some other entities exist too which possess unconscious bodies as well as conscious souls. Considering the fact that the *viruddhāvyabhicāra* relates to an independent and serious problem, it is by no means eccentric to even suppose that this doctrine had been developed by persons who were well acquainted with the SP but did not deem it worthy to take it into consideration, precisely because they, like the author of (E), thought that it would be 'ludicrous to assume' that this way of reasoning could validly establish any conclusion at all. It is hardly possible to concur with the suggestion in (E), p. 528, that, given that the SP was probably closer to Dharmakīrti's time 'the doctrinal element of *viruddhāvyabhicāra* was well known to its author'. Considering in addition that the transmission of information in those days must have been far slower than in the modern era and that even in most recent times various cases of plagiarism had been remained unnoticed for quite a long period and were detected merely with the help of advanced electronic devices, it has to be deemed 'ludicrous' to suppose that serious conclusions pertaining to relative chronology can be obtained by the available data. Accordingly, the only sober stance which can be taken (at present) is to confine oneself to assessments of theoretical relations between the SP and other doctrinal elements such as the *viruddhāvyabhicāra* in order to prevent unwarranted deductions concerning questions of dating.

The manner of treating the contention that the SP could have had (among others) the objective to establish a tenet of materialism is defective also in other respects. The criticism in (E) supports at best the conclusion that it is very improbable that its creator(s) or proponent(s) believed that they could prove the thesis of the existence of physical bodies endowed with consciousness by the reasoning contained in the SP alone. In this connection the propensity of the writer of (E) to take only those possibilities into account which come to his mind immediately or most easily turns out to be detrimental. It is well known — and attested in fairly old sources like the *Nyāyasūtra*s, the *Nyāyabhāṣya* and the *Vaiśeṣikasūtra*s — that in ancient times the view was current that the existence of an individual soul cannot be established by perception but by inference. In this situation it would not be inappropriate to argue for the tenet that phenomena of consciousness should be explained by the hypothesis of physical bodies manifesting them rather than by the postulation of souls by employing the strategy to invalidate *any* inferential proof for the existence of souls in combination with the conclusion that the pertinent issue can be decided *only* on the basis of perception — assuming that perception supports the materialist view. Since the SP, by showing that a form of reasoning complying with accepted standards of inferential validity can be made subservient for the derivation of any arbitrary tenet it serves the central purpose of discrediting at one blow all arguments trying to establish the thesis of the existence of souls.

The phenomenon that individual pieces of reasoning fulfil some overriding objective in the context of a more complex argumentative context is presumably not exceptional. For example, the individual pieces of reasoning employed in the first chapter of the

Mūlamadhyamakakārikā for refuting alternative possibilities of origination with the aim of establishing the possibility of origination in general exemplify an analogous embeddedness in a complex argumentative structure, and similar observations can be made elsewhere too. Thus it proves to be a plausible supposition that the SP incorporated from the very beginning a double function, i) a negative one of invalidating any inferences trying to prove the existence of souls and ii) a positive one of supporting a central tenet of materialism. There is admittedly no conclusive evidence vindicating this particular interpretation. But there is equally no conclusive evidence for the view adopted by Dharmakīrti according to which the SP should by itself provide a direct proof for the existence of bodies exhibiting consciousness. Exclusive acceptance of the latter alternative would need to resort to faith. To be sure, espousing the first option entails the admission that the SP can be connected with a criticism of inference, as it had been advocated in (A). However, the legitimacy and significance of this hypothesis has never been denied.

The second shortcoming of (D) is more important. The article has not merely failed to clearly point out the fact that the (customary) ascription of the SP to the 'materialists' is doubtful, but it was even contended, p. 507–508, that 'the piece of argument which is designated by the term *sadvitīyaprayoga* possesses considerable relevance for the assessment of the philosophical significance of schools of thought which were marginalized in the Indian tradition'. To be sure, the aim of emphasizing the potential relevance of 'marginalized' traditions is justified. But the presentation of the state of affairs as if the prejudice that the advocators of the SP were affiliated to the Cārvāka or Lokāyata tradition deserves to be uncritically accepted is definitely a major defect. It would have been appropriate to present the thesis explicitly in a conditional form by saying that if the proponents of the SP were representatives of some 'non-orthodox' tradition of thought then the SP vindicates the potential significance of those traditions and sustains the postulate to pay more attention to them than before.

The supposition that the inventor of the SP was not an adherent of some materialist or other non-orthodox school represents more than a mere conceivable possibility. For, if the conjecture that the SP was designed to throw a critical light on current accounts of inference is true, then the assumption that its conclusion represents a proposition that is not accepted in the milieu of its creator is at least as probable as the supposition that the conclusion is deemed to be true. After all, a criticism trying to establish that some variety or form of reasoning proves to be unreliable or invalid is most efficiently accomplished if it demonstrates that by employing the pertinent type of reasoning consequences are derivable which are patently unacceptable, i.e. either unacceptable for everybody or unacceptable for oneself and for those who share similar views.

To be sure, studies on Indian philosophies are apt to evoke the impression that exponents of that tradition are primarily concerned with criticizing other teachings but extremely reluctant to question themselves or critically analysing their own tradition. Nevertheless, the precept that criticism should not be interpreted as self-criticism can at best correspond to a fallible default-rule. Its indiscriminating application is extremely pernicious because it generates images of homogeneousness with respect to traditions or even entire cultures which are not grounded in objective facts but in methodological deficiencies. Even if one follows the suggestion advanced in (A) to the effect that the inventor(s) and proponent(s) of the SP intended to aim at a criticism of inference, the conclusion that he or they desired to 'show a serious deficiency in the structure of inference' and thereby to establish that 'inferences in general are unreliable' is not mandatory. As a matter of fact, there are at least three options:

a) The protagonist(s) of the SP intended indeed to argue for the thesis that 'inference should not be considered a reliable means of knowledge', as suggested in (A), p. 223.

b) The proponent(s) of the SP intended to show that some particular account of inference — such as the account presented by Vasubandhu — is (still) deficient and needs to be improved.

c) The originator(s) of the SP did not possess any clear awareness of the difference between a) and b), possibly presupposing that criticism of some particular account of inference amounts to criticism of inference in general.

The same exposition could be given *mutatis mutandis* with respect to the *pakṣasapakṣānyataratva*-argument. Among those options a) would imply that the inventor(s) of the SP failed to see that their argument was an inappropriate means to establish a far-reaching contention, b) would imply that they adopted a(n objectively) most reasonable stance and c) articulates a possibility which is quite realistic.

Thus it could be objected that the position advocated in (A), (C) and (E) according to which the SP was i) invented by an adherent of Lokāyata ii) created at a time between Dignāga and Dharmakīrti and iii) was meant to establish the thesis that inference should not be considered a reliable means of knowledge represents a possibility. But the crux lies in the circumstance that a possibility is passed off as a fact. It is problematic to endorse such a method which harmonizes with phenomena observable in the social media at present. Whereas (D) was guilty of paving a way for an uncritical acceptance of the prejudice that the SP possesses its origins in the milieu of the Cārvākas or Lokāyatas, (E), p. 527, goes much further by undertaking even the 'ludicrous' attempt to pass off this prejudice as an incontrovertible dogma, demanding that the SP *must* be assessed against the background of the 'Lokāyata tradition, with which the sp is affiliated'. Instead of circumspect consideration of possibilities the attitude of treating possibilities as facts deserves to be relentlessly repudiated. Fabrications of fake facts and pronouncements of exorbitant claims are in themselves less fatal than the consequences which they promote. By combining several premises of this sort the prospects of manufacturing complex webs of illusions are enhanced.

Postscript

At the end of FN a note occurred which read:

> [With the publication of this paper we hope to end this debate here. The Editor.]

Notwithstanding the circumstance that FN explicitly and extensively refers to (D) and indirectly relates to a discussion represented by four preceding articles concerning the topic of the *sadvitīyaprayoga* (= SP), the quoted remark failed to account for the fact that FN was not a mere continuation of the former debate, but shifted the topic to a different level of general matters of methodology. As it appeared apposite to inspect the legitimacy of the claims pertaining to new issues, an article was drafted by me taking a critical stand on a number of points articulated in FN, referring in various places to the topic of the SP for purposes of illustration. The first chapter of the present essay with the title "The Delusions of 'Historical Interpretation' " is a slightly extended version of that treatise.

Due to the circumstance that in this study the main focus lies on the general issues raised in FN, whereas the debate concerning the SP plays a subordinate role, a publication in the organ where FN as well as (A)–(C) had appeared would have been a natural option. Nevertheless, in view of the fact that — after almost a year of silence — the editor of the *Journal of Indian Philosophy* insisted on the standpoint articulated in the above cited quotation one is entitled to conclude that it had been decided from the outset that FN must not be exposed to further criticism. It is not even eccentric to surmise that the writer of FN could have chosen the specific presumptuous formulation for the title of his article in knowledge of this intention.

The query as to whether some individual article deserves to finalize particular discussions possesses only secondary importance relative to the general question regarding possible obligations entailed by the decision to terminate debates at some specific point. In this connection the following maxim amounts almost to a truism: A choice fixing an endpoint must not rely on quantitative considerations alone (such as number or length of articles devoted to some subject-matter) but needs to take into account qualitative aspects too. This implies that, whenever someone decides that some particular contribution to a topic should finalize its exploration for the moment, he must verify that the concerned contribution is suited to play this role also under qualitative aspects and if that is not the case see to it that it assumes a character which makes it suitable for that purpose. There can be hardly any doubt that those requirements have not been met in the present case.

As far as the specific study of the SP is concerned FN is badly suited for terminating investigations on that issue. But even if that were otherwise, the circumstance that FN raises bold claims relating to issues of methodology calls for critical opposition. In the second part of the present monograph, viz. in the segment with the title 'Retrospection', it has been attempted to demonstrate that notwithstanding the high implausibility of central contentions advanced in FN the article could be exploited as a suitable starting point for deeper explorations. One is entitled to presume that the identification of problematic aspects of previous discussions concerning the SP is apt to yield profits for structuring future debates concerning other topics too. If it has been envisaged that FN should mark the endpoint of previous discussions it would have been most appropriate to subject it to a careful review in order to achieve optimal improvements before publication. There can be no doubt that in this manner FN could have benefitted considerably. Even without being familiar with the specific topic of the SP a critical reviewer might, for example, have recognized the dubiousness of the dogmatic assumption that the SP *must* have been originated in the milieu of the Cārvāka or Lokāyata and pointed out that in this manner possibilities are passed off as facts. It could equally have been detected that observations to the effect that certain terms can be used to denote groups, collections, types or genera provide inconclusive evidence for the thesis that they must always be employed in this manner, since it is a pervasive phenomenon in natural languages that expressions denoting individuals or particulars can also denote groups, types or genera, and vice versa. Accordingly, with respect to specific tokens of linguistic types of this kind one must consider the plausibility of the resulting sense of the complex linguistic units containing them for making decisions concerning the actual import.[138] Far more significant is however the circumstance that FN is apt to induce serious confusions pertaining to different issues connected with investigations based on textual sources. Within the framework of a critical review it would have been apposite to call attention to the fact that the identification of some content and the assessment of various properties exhibited by a content constitute related but in principle different types of tasks. This is important because FN is not the only article revealing the absence of a clear awareness of the pertinent differences. The first task can be subdivided into a) textual criticism assessing some relevant wording and b) exegesis determining some or the other sort of sense, meaning or import connected with the pertinent wording as two components. Tasks of the second type can be guided by interests of philosophical analysis. But this is not necessarily so: Focus on properties of content could be equally motivated by an interest to find out what kind of thoughts were conceived by people at certain times, what strategies have been or could be used for persuading other people or using them for one's own interests etc.

---

[138] This can be easily seen with the help of the following very simple example. Let us suppose that somebody says:

'The following sentence
  Wine is not wine.
contains four words.'

Presuming reasonability on the part of the speaker one will interpret the expression 'words' as relating to word-tokens, whereas one would, on the same basis, assume that the expression ought to refer to word-types if 'three' had occurred instead of 'four'.

References

Franco, E. 2012. A Note on the *Sadvitīyaprayoga*. In: *Journal of Indian Philosophy* 40: 219–224. (= A)

—— 2013. Further notes on the *Sadvitīyaprayoga*. In: *Journal of Indian Philosophy* 41: 665–670 (= C)

—— 2016. Final Notes on the *Sadvitīyaprayoga*. In: *Journal of Indian Philosophy* 44: 525–535. (Published online: 16 May 2015. DOI 10.1007/s10781-015-9273-8) (= E)

Halbfass, W. 1997. *Arthakriyā* und *kṣaṇikatva*: Einige Beobachtungen. In: P. Kieffer-Pülz and J.-U. Hartmann (eds.), *Bauddhavidyāsudhākaraḥ: Studies in Honour of Heinz Bechert on the Occasion of His 65th Birthday*, Swisttal-Odendorf: Indica et Tibetica Verlag, pp. 233–247.

Hattiangadi, J.N. 1987. *How is Language Possible? Philosophical Reflections on the Evolution of Language and Knowledge*. La Salle, Illinois: Open Court Publishing.

Houben, J.E.M. 1995. Bhartṛhari's Solution to the Liar and Some Other Paradoxes. In: *Journal of Indian Philosophy* 23: 381–401.

Künne, W. 2013. *Epimenides und andere Lügner*. Frankfurt am Main: Klostermann Rote Reihe.

Lyons, J. 1969. *Introduction to Theoretical Linguistics*, Cambridge: Cambridge University Press.

Oetke, C. 2007. Some Aspects of Textual Exegesis with Regard to Dharmakīrti's Sattvānumāna. In: Karin Preisendanz (ed.), *Expanding and Merging Horizons. Contributions to South Asian and Cross-Cultural Studies in Commemoration of Wilhelm Halbfass*, (Beiträge zur Kultur- und Geistesgeschichte Asiens 53), Vienna: Austrian Academy of Sciences Press, pp. 571–584.

—— 2012. *Ascription of Linguistic Properties and Varieties of Content. Two Studies on Problems of Self-Reference*. Stockholm Universal Studies 20. Stockholm: Acta Universitatis Stockholmiensis.

—— 2013. A Brief Appraisal of the *Sadvitīyaprayoga*. In: *Journal of Indian Philosophy*, 41: 43–55. (= B)

—— 2013. Inconsistency, Paradox and Linguistic Content. Did Bhartṛhari offer a solution for Truth-Paradoxes. In: *Revista de Filosofía de la Universidad de Costa Rica* 52/134: 9–39.

—— 2016. Additional Notes on the *Sadvitīyaprayoga*. In: *Journal of Indian Philosophy* 44: 507–523. (= D)

—— 2016. Is the section of verses 1–29 in Vākyapadīya III.3 based on a sound theoretical motivation? In: *Revista Guillermo de Ockham* 14/1: 33–44. (DOI: http://dx.doi.org/10.21500/22563202.2314)